Easy Windows 95

Sue Plumley

Easy Windows 95

Copyright © 1995 by Que® Corporation

Library of Congress Catalog Card Number: 95-70647

International Standard Book Number: 1-56529-989-2

98 97 96 95   8 7 6 5 4 3 2 1

Interpretation of the printing code: the rightmost double-digit number is the year of the book's first printing; the rightmost single-digit number is the number of the book's printing. For example, a printing code of 95-1 shows that this copy of the book was printed during the first printing of the book in 1995.

Screen reproductions in this book were created by means of the program Collage Plus from Inner Media, Inc., Hollis, NH.

This book was produced digitally by Macmillan Computer Publishing and manufactured using 100% computer-to-plate technology (filmless process), by Shepard Poorman Communications Corporation, Indianapolis, Indiana.

Credits

Publisher
Roland Elgey

Vice President and Publisher
Marie Butler-Knight

Publishing Manager
Barry Pruett

Editorial Services Director
Elizabeth Keaffaber

Managing Editor
Michael Cunningham

Acquisitions Editor
Fred Slone

Product Development Specialist
Heather Stith

Production Editor
Kelly Oliver

Copy Editor
San Dee Phillips

Technical Editor
Richard F. Brown

Book Designers
Barbara Kordesh
Amy Peppler-Adams

Cover Designers
Dan Armstrong
Kim Scott

Production Team
Claudia Bell, Amy Cornwell,
Anne Dickerson, Karen Gregor-York,
Elizabeth Lewis, Clair Schweinler,
Mike Thomas, Suzanne Tulley,
Scott Tullis

Indexer
Carol Sheehan

Composed in *Stone Serif* and *MCPdigital* by Que Corporation

About the Author

Sue Plumley, who has a BA in Art, used her knowledge of design in desktop publishing and graphic art to manage the pre-press department of a commercial print shop before starting her own business seven years ago. Humble Opinions is a firm that specializes in consulting, training, and network installation, management, and maintenance. In the years since she began Humble Opinions, Sue has trained staff and employees of local companies, large corporations, and federal agencies in the use of various Microsoft applications, Microsoft Office, and other software programs, as well as offering support for the use of those products. In addition, Sue also taught the use of various software applications at Beckley College in Beckley, West Virginia. Finally, Sue has written and contributed to over thirty books about computer software for Que and its sister imprints.

Acknowledgments

I'd like to thank all the people at Que who worked to make this project successful. I'm grateful to Heather Stith and Kelly Oliver for their advice and guidance. I'd also like to thank Martha O'Sullivan for her expedient and unwavering assistance in all things associated with this book. Finally, all my thanks to my husband, Carlos, for his patience and love.

Trademark Acknowledgments

All terms mentioned in this book that are known to be, or are suspected of being, trademarks or service marks have been appropriately capitalized. Que Corporation cannot attest to the accuracy of this information. Use of a term in this book should not be regarded as affecting the validity of any trademark or service mark.

Contents

Part VII: Personalizing Windows　　174

Part VIII: Sharing Data with Windows　　196

Part IX: Using Windows Accessories　　212

Part X: Maintaining Windows 95　　240

Index　　258

Introduction

Windows has always been an amazing graphical environment. Windows 95 advances utility and facility so that whether you are a beginning or advanced user, you can benefit from the new features, interface, networking capabilities, and so on. Using Windows 95, you can start and operate one or more applications easily and efficiently, as well as switch between applications effortlessly. Additionally, you can share information between applications, customize the interface, manage and print files with ease, and perform many other tasks using the improved user interface and features.

Specifically, you can use Windows 95 to accomplish the following:

- *Manipulate windows.* Using the mouse, you can move a window around on the *desktop*—the background on which windows and icons appear—and resize any window. Additionally, you can arrange windows on the desktop, reduce or minimize a window, maximize a window, and so on. The control you have over the physical size and placement of the various windows enables you to work in your own way.

- *Manage files and folders.* Windows uses *folders*—representing directories—to hold files you use in your work. You can create new folders to hold files; open and close folders for viewing; and move, copy, rename and delete folders to help organize your computer's directories and subdirectories. In addition, you can manage files by viewing, sorting, copying, moving, renaming, and so on.

- *Use Windows' extensive Help features.* Windows provides an excellent Help feature that enables you to search for specific topics, view procedures, locate terms, and otherwise find the help you need to perform tasks in Windows. Windows also offers a handy shortcut feature that lets you quickly open documents, files, or folders by bypassing the menus and dialog boxes.

■ *Control applications.* You can use both Windows and DOS programs within Windows, and you can start a program with Windows. You can also easily install new software applications and create folders to hold the programs.

■ *Print from Windows.* Print documents from Windows applications, use the print queue to arrange printing priority, select and use a default printer, add other printers to the setup, change settings and options, pause and restart the print job, and more.

■ *Control Windows fonts.* You can change the size and typeface of the Windows display fonts. Windows also enables you to insert symbols and other special characters into documents and other files. Additionally, you can use the Windows Font Manager to add and delete fonts, print samples of fonts, and so on.

■ *Personalize Windows.* Windows provides the means to customize Windows features such as screen colors, mouse movements and speed, and passwords; it also enables you to easily change the system time and date.

■ *Share information.* Windows enables you to easily switch between open programs so you can work in more than one file at a time. Furthermore, you can copy and move data in any application to another application and *link* data so that modified information is automatically updated from program to program.

■ *Use Windows accessories.* Windows provides many accessories, or programs, you can use. WordPad is a word processor; there's also a calendar, calculator, paint program, and several games for your amusement.

■ *Maintain your system.* Use Wizards to notify Windows of newly installed hardware, clean up your disk (hard or floppy) by defragmenting it, and scan disks for damage using ScanDisk.

Task Sections

The Task sections of this book include numbered steps that tell you how to accomplish certain tasks, such as opening an application, arranging windows on the desktop, or writing and editing text in WordPad. The numbered steps walk you through a specific example so you can learn the task by actually doing it.

Big Screen

At the beginning of each task is a large screen that usually shows how the computer screen will look after you complete the procedure that follows in that task. Sometimes, however, the screen shot shows a feature discussed in the task, such as a shortcut menu.

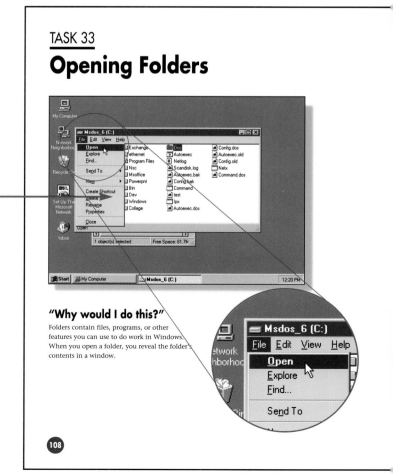

TASK 33

Opening Folders

"Why would I do this?"

Folders contain files, programs, or other features you can use to do work in Windows. When you open a folder, you reveal the folder's contents in a window.

108

Notes

Many tasks include short notes that tell you a little more about certain procedures. These notes define terms, explain other options, refer you to other sections when applicable, and so on.

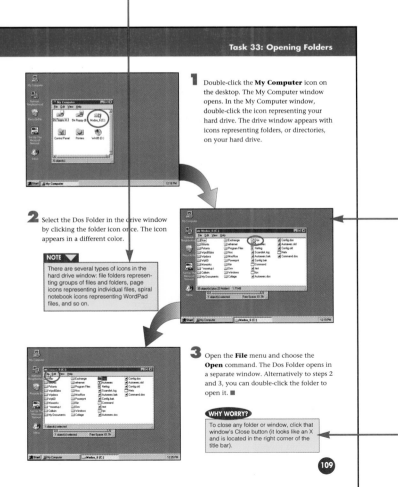

Task 33: Opening Folders

1 Double-click the **My Computer** icon on the desktop. The My Computer window opens. In the My Computer window, double-click the icon representing your hard drive. The drive window appears with icons representing folders, or directories, on your hard drive.

2 Select the Dos Folder in the drive window by clicking the folder icon once. The icon appears in a different color.

NOTE
There are several types of icons in the hard drive window: file folders representing groups of files and folders, page icons representing individual files, spiral notebook icons representing WordPad files, and so on.

3 Open the **File** menu and choose the **Open** command. The Dos Folder opens in a separate window. Alternatively to steps 2 and 3, you can double-click the folder to open it. ■

WHY WORRY?
To close any folder or window, click that window's Close button (it looks like an X and is located in the right corner of the title bar).

109

Step-by-Step Screens

Each task includes a screen shot for each step of a procedure. The screen shot shows how the computer screen looks at each step in the process.

Why Worry? Notes

You may find that you performed a task (such as creating a folder) that you did not want to do after all. The Why Worry? notes tell you how to undo certain procedures or get out of a situation, such as displaying a Help screen or closing a window.

PART I
Controlling Windows

Before you can use Windows 95, you must have it installed on your computer. Many computers come with Windows 95 already installed; if yours doesn't, follow these steps:

To install Windows 95 on a stand-alone computer:

1. Place the CD in the drive. In DOS, type the letter of the CD drive and press **Enter**.

2. Type **setup** and press **Enter**. Windows runs ScanDisk, a diagnostic tool, to check your disk for problems. Follow any directions and answer any questions when prompted by ScanDisk.

3. The Setup Options window appears. Choose from one of the following setup options: Typical (most common components), Portable (choose for a notebook computer), Compact (saves space by installing only necessary components), or Custom (choose your own components; recommended only for advanced users). Select an option and choose **Next**.

4. In the User Info window, enter your name and company and choose **Next**.

5. In the Product ID window, enter your ID number and choose **Next**.

6. In the Analyzing Computer window, check any items you have in your system, such as sound, MIDI, or video capture card. Choose **Next**.

7. In the Get Connected dialog box, choose the components you want to install: The Microsoft Network, Microsoft Mail, Microsoft Fax. Choose **Next**.

8. In the Windows Components window, choose whether to install common components such as games, disk tools, and so on. Choose **Next**.

9. In the Identification window, enter a Computer Name, Workgroup name, and Computer description. Choose **Next**.

10. The Startup Disk window appears. Choose whether to create a startup disk or not. Choose **Next**.

11. Windows begins copying files from the startup disk to your computer. Place a disk in the drive when prompted and choose **OK**. When prompted, remove disk and click **OK**.

12. Windows begins to copy files. During the process, various screens containing information about Windows appear and a progress bar displays at the bottom of the screen.

13. Copying takes anywhere between 30–60 minutes, depending on the speed of your computer. When Setup finishes copying files, it displays the Finishing Setup window. Choose **Finish**.

14. Windows reboots the computer and starts Windows. A message appears: **Getting ready to run Windows 95 for the first time...** . Windows takes several minutes to prepare.

15. Windows displays a message that it is setting up your hardware, programs, Control Panel, Help, Time Zone, and MS-DOS program settings; this takes several minutes.

16. Windows displays the Date/Time Properties dialog box. In the Time Zone tab, make sure your time zone is listed; in the Date & Time tab, make sure the correct month, year, date, and time are listed. If any of the information is wrong, enter the correct data and choose **Close**.

17. Windows finalizes the setup and displays the Welcome to Windows 95 dialog box>. You can choose to take a tour, see what's new, register online, or close the window. You're done.

After you install Windows 95, you will see a screen called the desktop. From the desktop, you can open and switch between applications, search for specific folders, print documents, and perform other tasks. (To effectively accomplish these tasks, you must know how to use a mouse; the first task in this part explains how.) The following list explains the parts of the desktop:

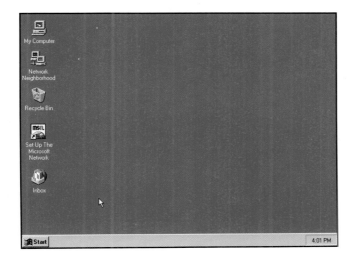

- The *My Computer* window holds icons representing your computer's drives and directories, the Control Panel, and the Printers folder. You will learn how to manipulate the My Computer window in this part. Part IV explains how to use the My Computer window to manage your files.

- The *Start button* provides a menu offering quick access to programs, documents, settings, help topics, and so on.

- The *taskbar* is a horizontal bar located along the bottom of the screen that displays the Start menu and lists the open applications and documents. You can show or hide the taskbar, and you can even move it from its original spot to make your work easier. This part explains how to perform these tasks.

- *Network Neighborhood* is a window that displays the computers on the network, if you are connected to a network, such as a file server containing shared folders.

- *The Microsoft Network* is an online service in which you can exchange messages with others; read news, sports, and weather; find technical information; and connect to the Internet.

- The *Inbox* is a feature that enables you to send and receive faxes (the Inbox appears only if you installed Microsoft Exchange).

- You'll also see *windows* on the desktop. They are rectangular areas on-screen containing folders, files, documents, dialog boxes, messages, and so on. You can easily move, size, and manipulate the windows to organize your desktop to suit your working routine. You open windows to view and make use of the items and applications within them.

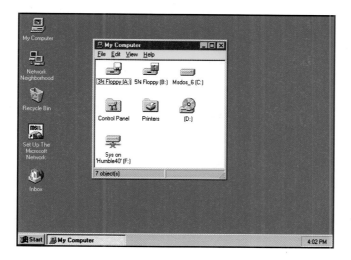

When you finish working for the day, you must shut down Windows before you turn off your computer, so you do not lose any unsaved data or files. This part explains how to do this.

TASK 1
Using the Mouse

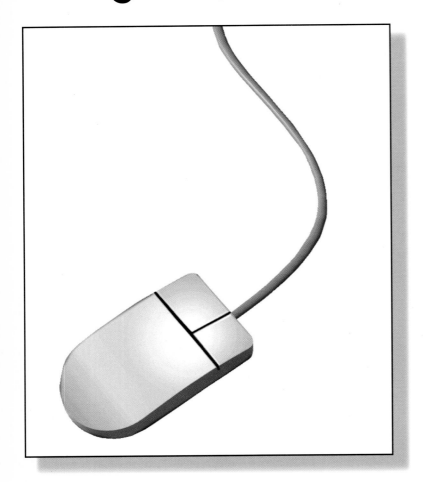

"Why would I do this?"

Windows presents information in a visual way so you can easily access what you need without having to memorize a lot of commands and keystrokes. To effectively use Windows, you need to learn how to use the mouse. The mouse is a small device that has two or more buttons and connects to your computer. This task explains how you can manipulate different Windows elements by moving the mouse on your desk and by pressing the buttons.

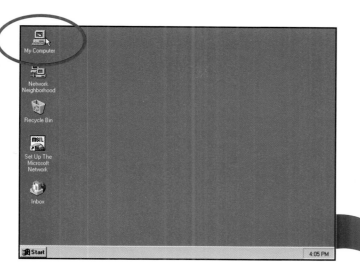

1 Move the mouse on your desk until its corresponding on-screen pointer is on the picture labeled **My Computer**. This action is called *pointing*. On-screen pictures (such as the one labeled **My Computer**) are called *icons*.

2 Press and release the left mouse button to select the icon. The selected icon appears in a different color or in reversed video. Pressing and releasing the left mouse button is called *clicking*.

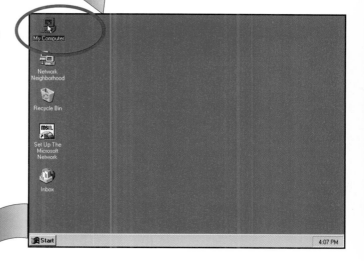

> **NOTE** ▼
>
> Sometimes, you need to press the right mouse button to perform a task. In this case, I'll tell you to click with the right mouse button. (Clicking the right mouse button usually makes a pop-up window or menu appear.)

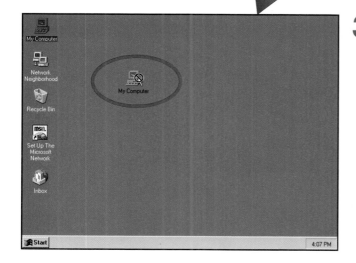

3 Press the left mouse button again, but this time don't release it. While holding down the left mouse button, move the mouse across your desk. This action is called *dragging*. As you drag, notice a ghost of the icon moves with your mouse pointer on-screen. Release the mouse button, and the icon moves to the pointer's position. To move the My Computer icon back to its original position, click the icon and drag it with the mouse.

4 Point to the **My Computer** icon and quickly press and release the left mouse button two times. This action is called *double-clicking*. The My Computer icon opens the window it represents. Double-clicking icons and folders in Windows opens that window, program, drive, or document. To close the window, click the **Close** button (**X**) in the top right corner of the window. ■

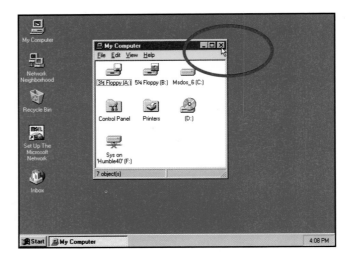

Mouse Moves Review

Point	Move your mouse so its corresponding on-screen pointer touches the item you want to select.
Click	Press and release the left mouse button after positioning the on-screen mouse pointer.
Drag	Hold down the left mouse button and move the mouse across your desk until the on-screen pointer and the selected item are in the position you want. Then release the mouse button.
Double-click	Press and release the left mouse button twice in quick succession.

Using the Start Button

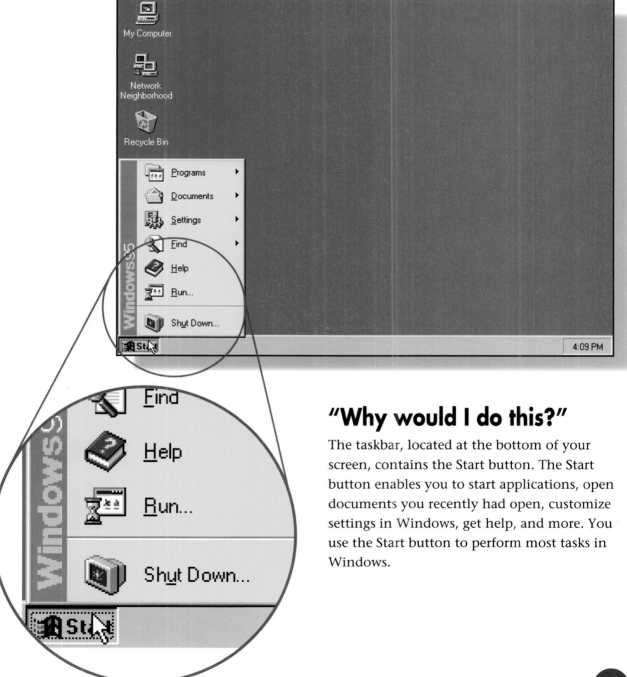

"Why would I do this?"

The taskbar, located at the bottom of your screen, contains the Start button. The Start button enables you to start applications, open documents you recently had open, customize settings in Windows, get help, and more. You use the Start button to perform most tasks in Windows.

15

1 Point to the **Start** button on the taskbar with the mouse pointer, and then click the left mouse button. As you point to the button, a pop-up help bubble briefly appears, saying, **Click here to start**. The Start menu appears.

> **NOTE** ▼
>
> Commands followed by an arrow (>) display a secondary menu; commands followed by an ellipsis (...) display a related dialog box.

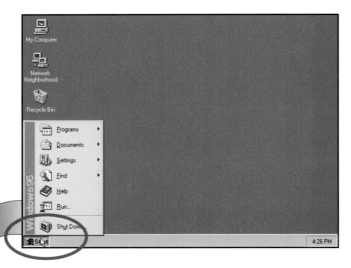

2 Move the mouse pointer to the Programs command to display a secondary menu of folders containing applications; for example, the Accessories folder contains Windows applications such as WordPad, Games, Calculator, Calendar, and so on.

> **NOTE** ▼
>
> Your programs list may include many other folders that contain programs, such as Microsoft Office Applications, Lotus Applications, MS Works, and so on.

3 Point the mouse pointer at the **Accessories** folder to display a menu of programs in the folder. If you wanted to open one of the programs, you would point to the program name and click. For now, click on the desktop to close the Start menu. ■

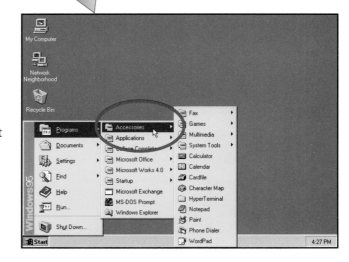

Opening a Window

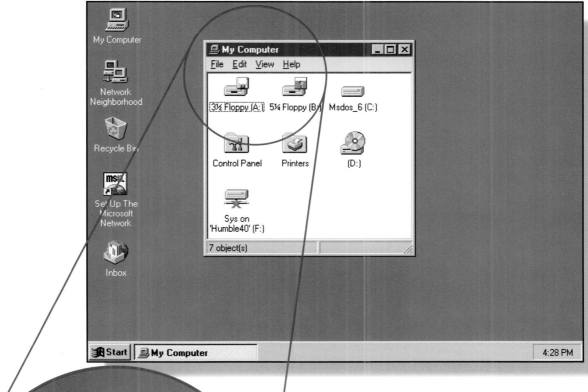

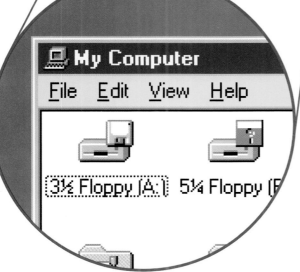

"Why would I do this?"

Windows 95 displays all of its information in on-screen boxes called *windows*. Before you can work with any of the information on your computer, you must know how to display (or *open*) these windows. In a previous task, "Using the Mouse," you opened the My Computer window by double-clicking its icon. This task describes an alternative method of opening windows.

1 Point at the **My Computer** icon with the mouse pointer.

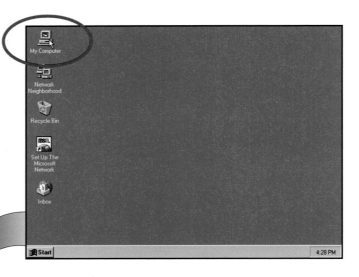

2 Click the right mouse button to display the icon's quick menu. Click the word **Open** with the left mouse button to choose that command. The My Computer window opens.

NOTE ▼

Quick menus are shortcut menus that offer common commands related to the object you right-click. Try right-clicking the mouse on the taskbar and on the desktop to see the quick menus related to those items. To cancel a quick menu, click the left mouse button on the desktop.

3 Note that a button for the My Computer window appears on the taskbar next to the Start button. ■

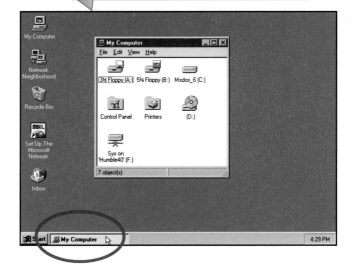

Reducing and Enlarging a Window

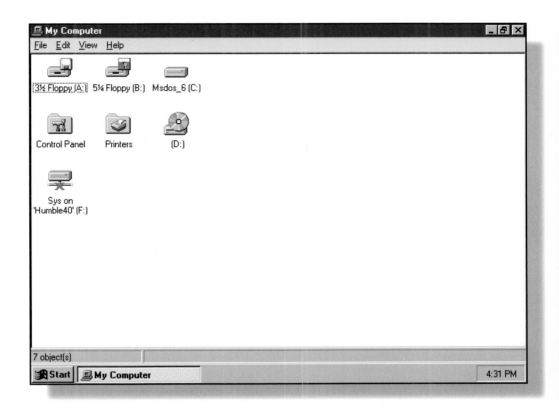

"Why would I do this?"

You can reduce (*minimize*) or enlarge (*maximize*) program and document windows to make your work easier. Minimize a window to move it out of your way temporarily while leaving it active for later use. Maximize a window so you can see more of its contents on-screen.

1 With the **My Computer** window open, point the mouse at the **Minimize** button—the button with an underline (_) located in the upper right corner of the title bar—and click the left mouse button. The window disappears from the desktop and its button on the taskbar appears raised instead of recessed.

> **NOTE** ▼
>
> All application and document windows have Minimize and Maximize buttons.

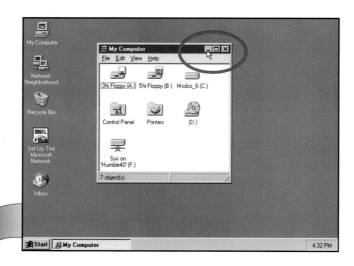

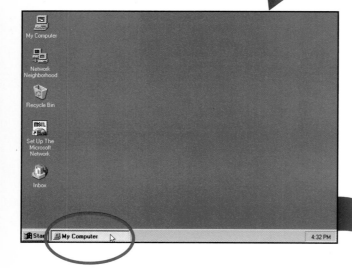

2 Point at the **My Computer** button on the taskbar with the mouse pointer and click the left mouse button. The My Computer window opens.

> **NOTE** ▼
>
> When you point the mouse at a button—and often at toolbars and other icons in Windows—a ToolTip appears. A ToolTip is a small box containing the name of the program or tool represented by the button.

3 Point at the **Maximize** button—the button containing a rectangle in the upper right corner of the title bar of the My Computer window—and click the left mouse button. The window enlarges to fill the screen and the Maximize button changes to the Restore button.

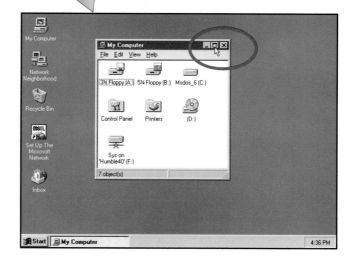

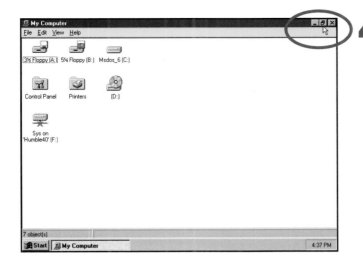

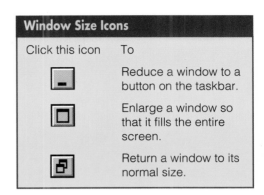

4 Click the **Restore** button to change the window back to its original size. ■

Window Size Icons

Click this icon	To
	Reduce a window to a button on the taskbar.
	Enlarge a window so that it fills the entire screen.
	Return a window to its normal size.

Moving and Resizing a Window

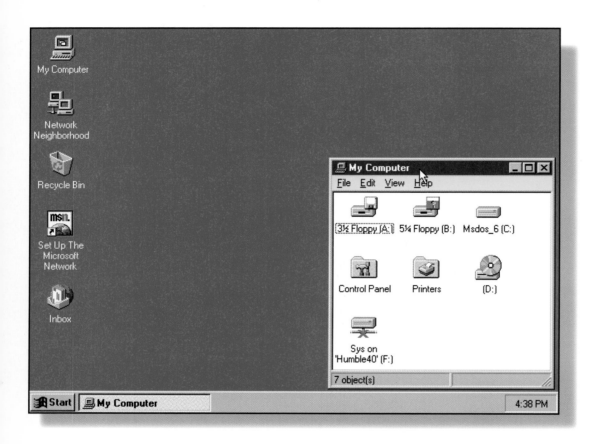

"Why would I do this?"

As you add more applications, folders, short-cuts, and so on, to the desktop, you'll need more room to display these elements. Resize a window to save room on the desktop and move the windows so you can see all the open windows at one time.

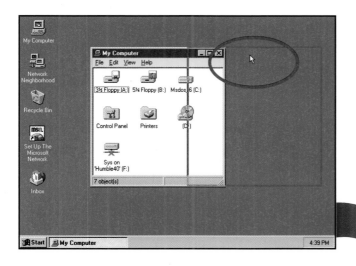

1 To move any open window, point anywhere in the title bar, and then click and drag the window to a new position. The window border moves with the mouse pointer; when you release the mouse button, the window and its contents appear in the new location.

NOTE ▼

Unless otherwise specified, when I tell you to click, point, or drag, you should use the left, or primary, mouse button.

2 Position the mouse pointer over any one window border until a double-headed arrow appears. Drag toward the center of the window to reduce the size, or drag away from the center to enlarge the size. You can also drag a corner of the window to resize both dimensions at one time.

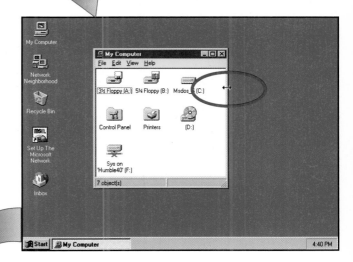

3 If the window is too small to show all of the contents of the window, horizontal and/or vertical scroll bars appear. Click the arrow at either end of a scroll bar to view the hidden contents of the window; scrolling lets you view different items in a too-small window. ■

NOTE ▼

To use a scroll bar, click the arrow at one end of the scroll bar. Additionally, you can click the mouse anywhere on the scroll bar to move around the window.

23

Using Menus

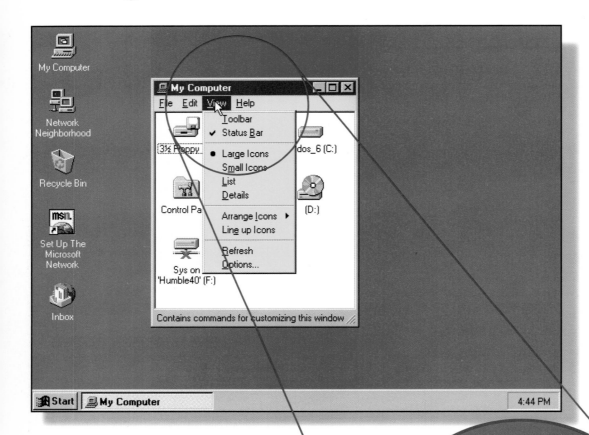

"Why would I do this?"

Although you can perform many tasks by clicking the mouse on different on-screen objects, you need to choose commands to perform the majority of Windows tasks. Commands are organized in *menus* to make them easy to find. In the task "Opening a Window," for example, you displayed a quick menu from which you chose the Open command. Most windows contain *menu bars* across the top of the window that list the available menus and each menu contains related commands.

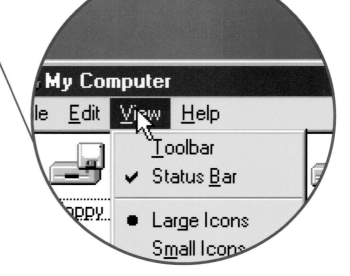

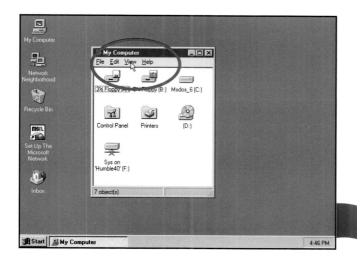

1 Open the **My Computer** window. Notice the list of menus across the top of the window. Point at the word **View** with the mouse pointer and click the left mouse button. The View menu opens.

NOTE ▼

The Control menu, located in the top left corner of the title bar, contains commands related to the open window, such as Restore, Move, Size, Close, and so on. Access the Control menu by clicking the icon in the title bar.

2 Click **Small Icons** to choose the command and close the menu. The icons in the My Computer window change to small icons. (To change them back, open the **View** menu and choose the **Large Icons** command.) ■

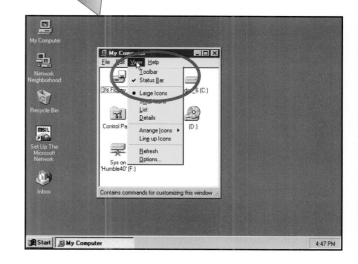

Reading a Menu

What You May See on a Menu	What It Means
Keyboard shortcut to the right of a command	Press the shortcut keys instead of accessing the menu the next time you want to perform that command.
Check mark	The command is active; for example, the check beside the View, Status Bar command means the status bar is showing in the window. More than one command on a menu may have a check mark next to it. Click a command to display the check mark and click it again to remove the check mark.

Reading a Menu Continued

What You May See on a Menu	What It Means
A dot to the left of a command	Shows a command has been selected. Only one command in a menu may be selected at a time, if dots appear beside the commands. Click a command to display the dot, and click another in the group to remove the dot.
An arrow to the right of a command	More options are available. Point to the command with an arrow following it and a secondary menu appears from which you can choose more commands.
An ellipsis after a command	A dialog box containing more options will appear if you choose that command.

Changing the Window Display

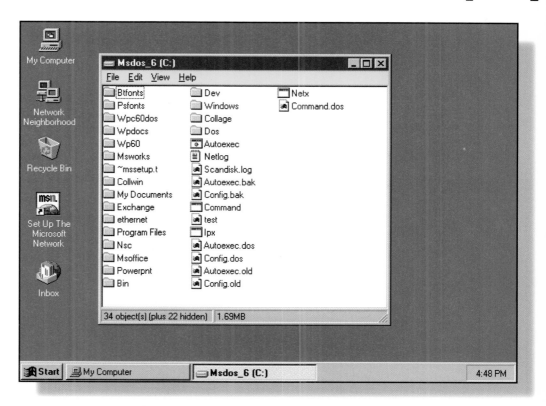

"Why would I do this?"

In Windows, you can view the contents of a window in a variety of ways. By default, Windows uses large icons to display the contents of a window. If you want to see more of a window's contents at one time, you can change the view to small icons (as discussed in the previous task). You can also display details such as type, size, and the date the item was last modified. (You can also sort the contents of the window by these details.) Changing the way a window displays its contents can make it easier to find what you need.

1 In the My Computer window, open your hard drive by double-clicking the icon. Open the **View** menu and click the **Details** command. The window now displays elements in list form. You may need to enlarge the window to view all the file details.

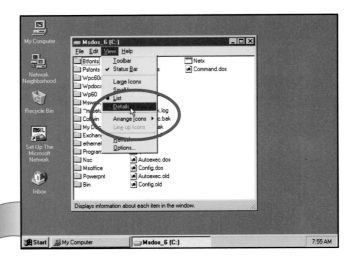

2 Open the **View** menu and choose **Arrange Icons**. A secondary menu appears; choose **by Date**. The folders and files in the window are rearranged by the last date they were modified.

3 To change back to the original view, open the **View** menu and click the **List** command. You can resize the window if necessary. ■

WHY WORRY?

You can rearrange the icons in the window by dragging each one to a new location. If the icons will not move, open the View menu and click the Arrange Icons command, and then (from the sec-ondary menu) choose Auto Arrange so the check mark disappears from this option.

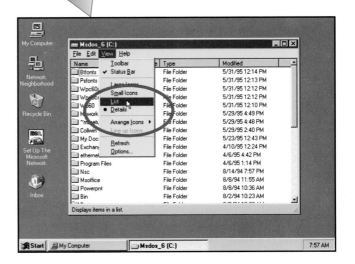

Arranging Windows on the Desktop

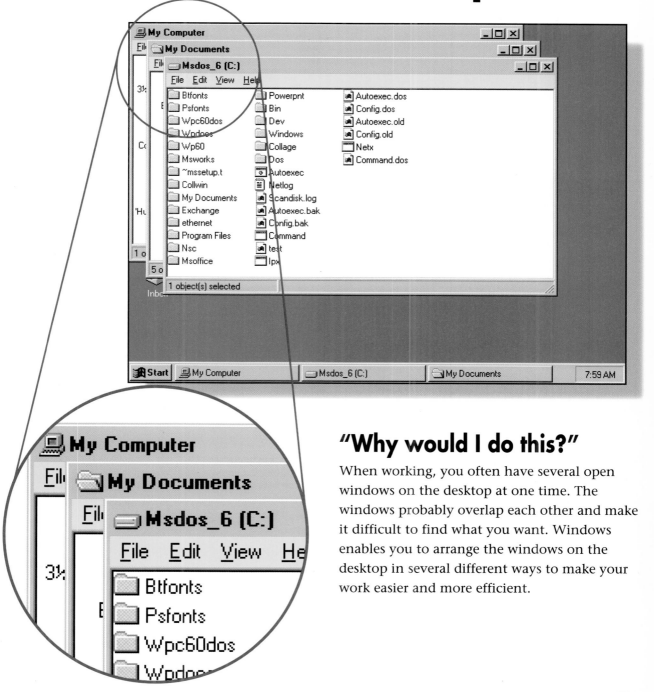

"Why would I do this?"

When working, you often have several open windows on the desktop at one time. The windows probably overlap each other and make it difficult to find what you want. Windows enables you to arrange the windows on the desktop in several different ways to make your work easier and more efficient.

1 Open multiple windows on the desktop. Point to an area on the taskbar that is not covered with a button or the time, and then press the right mouse button to reveal the quick menu.

WHY WORRY?

If you have trouble finding an unoccupied space on the taskbar, you can enlarge the bar as you would enlarge a window. To enlarge the taskbar, position the mouse pointer on the bar's border until you see a double-headed arrow; then drag the border up to enlarge the bar.

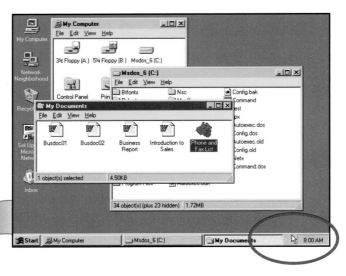

2 From the quick menu, choose **Cascade** to display the windows in an orderly fashion. Windows arranges the open windows to overlap and resizes them so they are all the same size. To work in any window, click the mouse in that window to make it *active*. An active window moves to the front of the rest, and its title bar is a different color.

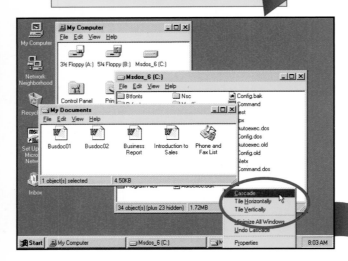

3 Click the right mouse button on the taskbar and choose **Tile Horizontally** or **Tile Vertically** to rearrange the open windows in a different way. ■

NOTE ▼

In addition to arranging the windows on the desktop, you can also resize a window or move it after you rearrange, as described in the task "Moving and Resizing a Window."

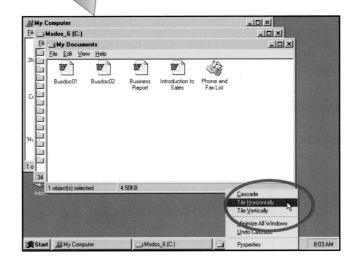

Closing Windows

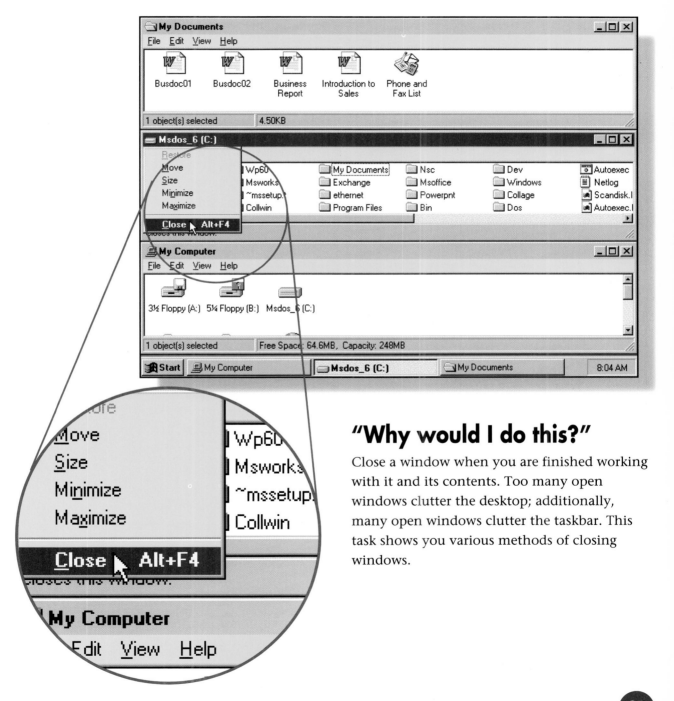

"Why would I do this?"

Close a window when you are finished working with it and its contents. Too many open windows clutter the desktop; additionally, many open windows clutter the taskbar. This task shows you various methods of closing windows.

1 You can close a window by clicking the **Close** button (X) in the right corner of the window's title bar.

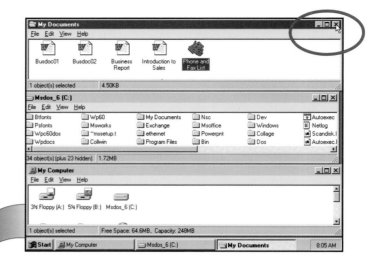

2 You can close a window by clicking the **Control-menu box** in the right corner of the title bar to open the Control menu and then choosing the **Close** command.

NOTE ▼

As a shortcut to close a window, select the window and press Alt+F4. Another shortcut is to double-click the Control-menu box.

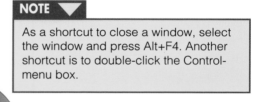

3 You can also close a window by selecting the window, opening the **File** menu, and then choosing the **Close** command. ■

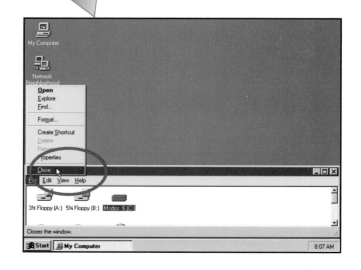

Using a Dialog Box

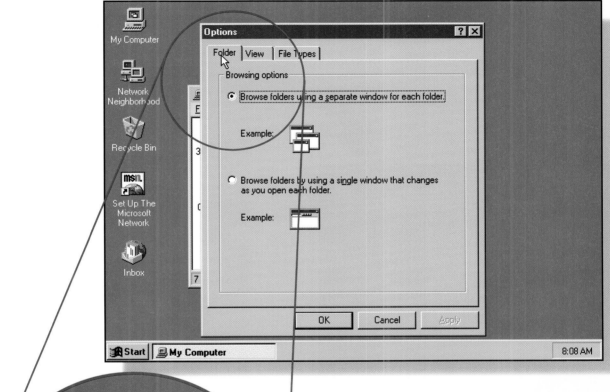

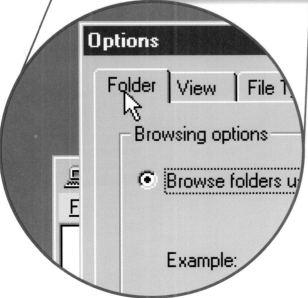

"Why would I do this?"

Dialog boxes contain options from which you
can choose to control windows, applications,
document formatting, and a host of other
procedures. Dialog boxes are widespread in
Windows; luckily, all dialog boxes have
common elements and all are treated in a
similar way. This task shows you how to open
and maneuver a dialog box.

1 In the My Computer window, select the **View** menu and choose **Options**. A command with an ellipsis following it means that command leads to a dialog box containing more related options.

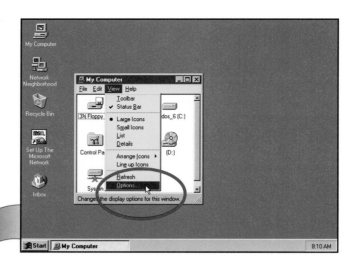

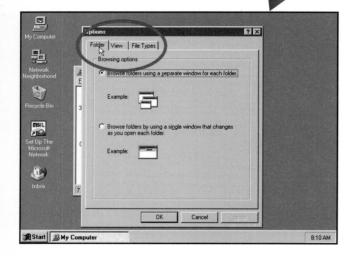

2 The Options dialog box appears. This particular dialog box contains three tabs which hold information and options relating to viewing windows as well as some features common to all dialog boxes. To view a tab's contents, click the tab. The following table describes options available in most dialog boxes. ■

NOTE ▼

When a dialog box is open, you cannot perform any other actions until you either accept changes by choosing OK or cancel the dialog box. A shortcut for accepting changes in a dialog box is to press the Enter key; a shortcut for canceling the box is to press the Esc key.

Element	Description
Tabs	"Pages" within the dialog box that include specific options and information related to the dialog box. To view a tab, click it.
Option buttons	Round white buttons that contain a black dot when selected. Choose an option to activate it. You can only choose one option in a group of options; choosing a second option deselects the first.
List boxes	Lists of available items (such as files) that you can scroll through and select from. Select an item by clicking it.
Check boxes	Square boxes that indicate options. Select the option by clicking it; a check mark appears in the square box. You can check one or more check box options in a group.
Text boxes	Boxes in which you can enter a measurement, such as point sizes for fonts.
Command buttons	Common buttons include OK and Cancel. Click OK to accept the changes you made in a dialog box, and click Cancel to cancel all changes and close the dialog box. Other command buttons may lead you to another dialog box or may perform an action.

Showing and Hiding the Taskbar

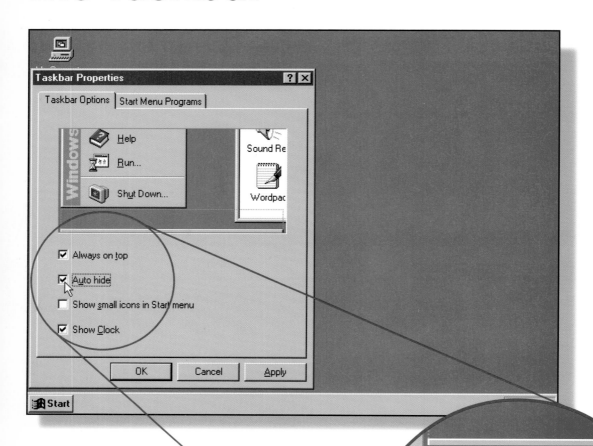

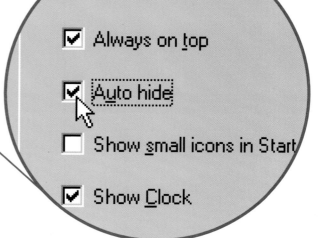

"Why would I do this?"

Windows' default is to show the taskbar at all times in the desktop. You can, however, hide the taskbar so you have more room on the desktop for other windows, folders, and programs. When you hide the taskbar, it disappears while you are working in a window and then reappears when you minimize or close that particular window. This task describes how to hide the taskbar.

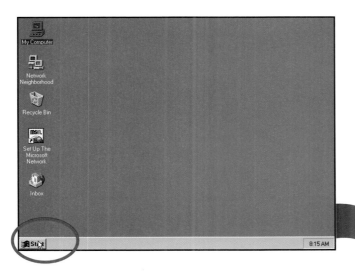

1 Click the **Start** button on the taskbar. The Start menu appears.

2 Choose the **Settings** command; a secondary menu appears. Choose **Taskbar**. The Taskbar Properties window appears.

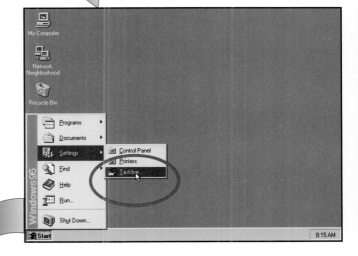

3 Click the **Taskbar Options** tab to display it, if it is not already showing.

37

4 In the Taskbar Options tab, click the **Auto hide** check box. Clicking the box adds a check mark to indicate the option is active. If you click the box again, the check mark disappears and the option becomes deactivated. Click the **OK** button to accept the changes you made to the Taskbar Options tab. The window closes and the taskbar disappears.

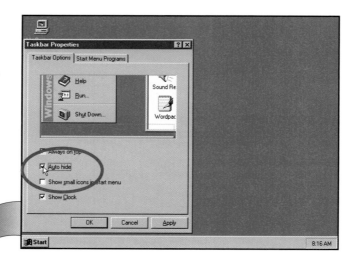

5 To show the taskbar while working, move the mouse to the bottom of the screen. The taskbar appears so you can choose applications or documents.

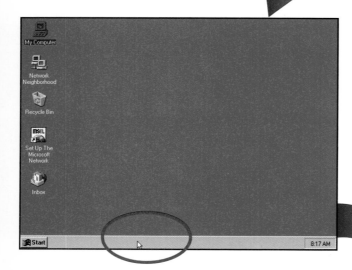

6 When you move the mouse away from the bottom of the screen, the taskbar disappears again. ■

WHY WORRY?

If you would prefer to show the taskbar at all times, open the Start menu and choose the Settings command. From the secondary menu, choose the Taskbar command. In the Taskbar Options tab, click the Auto hide option to remove the check mark and then choose OK to accept the change and close the dialog box.

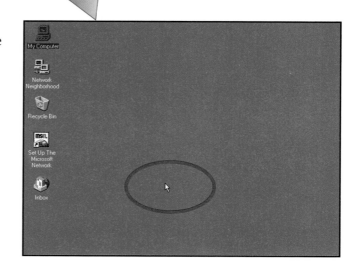

TASK 12
Moving and Resizing the Taskbar

"Why would I do this?"

Windows enables you to move the taskbar to the top, left, or right of the screen so the desktop is more comfortable for your working style. You can try moving the taskbar to various areas on the screen, and then you can choose the area you like best. This task illustrates how to move the taskbar.

1 Position the mouse pointer anywhere on the taskbar except on a button or the time.

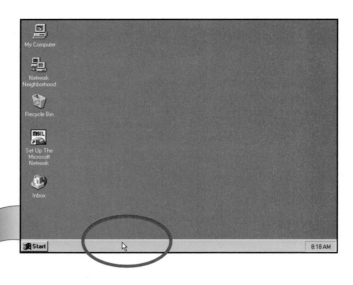

2 Drag the taskbar up and to the right. The taskbar's border moves with the mouse; when you release the mouse button, the taskbar jumps to the new location.

WHY WORRY?

To move the taskbar back to the bottom of the screen, drag it to that area.

3 To resize the taskbar, position the mouse pointer on one of the taskbar's borders until you see the double-headed arrow. Drag the arrow to resize the taskbar. ■

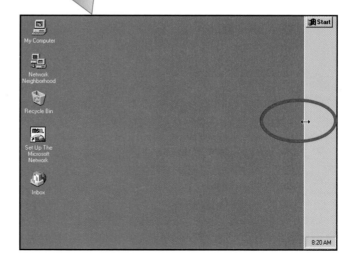

Shutting Down the Computer

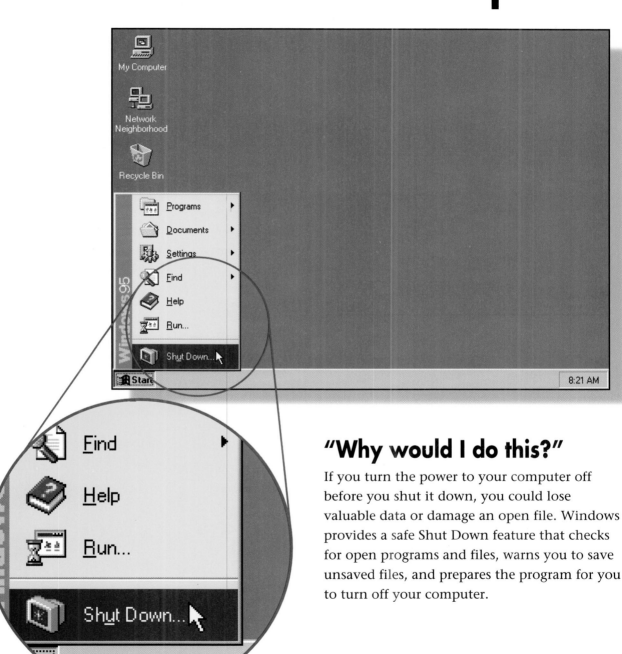

"Why would I do this?"

If you turn the power to your computer off before you shut it down, you could lose valuable data or damage an open file. Windows provides a safe Shut Down feature that checks for open programs and files, warns you to save unsaved files, and prepares the program for you to turn off your computer.

1 Before shutting down the computer, close all open programs. You may also want to close open windows and folders, although it is not necessary.

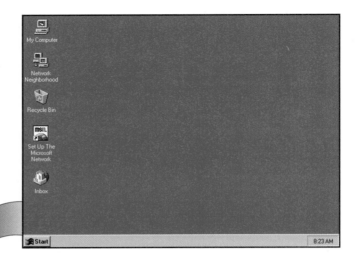

2 Open the **Start** menu and click **Shut Down**. Windows checks the system and prepares for the shut down. Windows displays the Shut Down Windows dialog box.

NOTE ▼

Often, you need to work from DOS instead of Windows. Windows 95 provides an easy way to boot to DOS. When you choose Shut Down, the Shut Down Windows dialog box appears. In the Are you sure you want to list, choose the Restart the computer in MS-DOS mode option and then choose Yes.

3 The default selection in the Shut Down Windows dialog box is **Shut down the computer?** Click the **Yes** button to complete the task. Windows displays a final screen that tells you when it is safe to turn off the power to your computer. ■

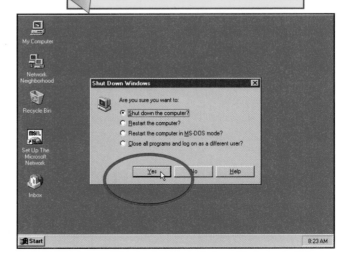

PART II

Getting Help

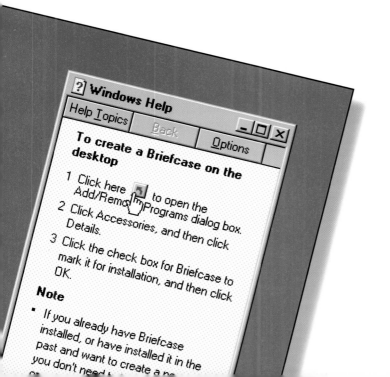

Windows provides various Help features to help you perform complex and everyday tasks such as using icons, inserting information, installing hardware and software, locating files, using the mouse, moving files, and so on.

When you initiate the Help feature from the Start menu, the Help window appears. From the Help window, you have three different ways to find the information you want: Contents, Index, and Find. Contents lists general topics such as Introducing Windows, Tour: Ten minutes to using Windows, How To..., and so on. The Index lists all Help topics; enter a topic and the index moves to that Help entry. In Find, type a word you want to find and a list of related topics appears.

When you choose a topic, Help displays a window describing how to perform the task or use the feature step by step. Help windows are like any other window; they include borders, Minimize and Maximize buttons, a Control-menu box, and so on. Additionally, you can move, resize, and close Help windows. Refer to Part I if you need instruction on how to manipulate windows.

Included in many of the Help topics are shortcuts that lead directly to a dialog box or application; for example, in the Help window explaining how to use the Briefcase, one step offers a "click here" shortcut that enables you to create a Briefcase for immediate use.

In conjunction with the Help feature, you can add annotations, or notes, to any feature to remind you of information that might be helpful the next time you access the topic. When you add an annotation, Windows displays a paper clip beside the topic in the topic's window. Click on the paper clip and Windows displays your comments. Another handy advantage of the Help feature is that you can print any Help topic for easy reference.

In addition to the Help topics, Windows includes other forms of assistance. *ToolTips* are handy pop-up boxes that describe tools and buttons within the program. They appear when you point at a tool with the mouse pointer. Windows also provides a context-sensitive tool called *What's This?*, which appears as a question mark button in dialog boxes. When you click the question mark, you can then click any item in the dialog box for descriptions and definitions of that item or option.

TASK 14

Starting Help

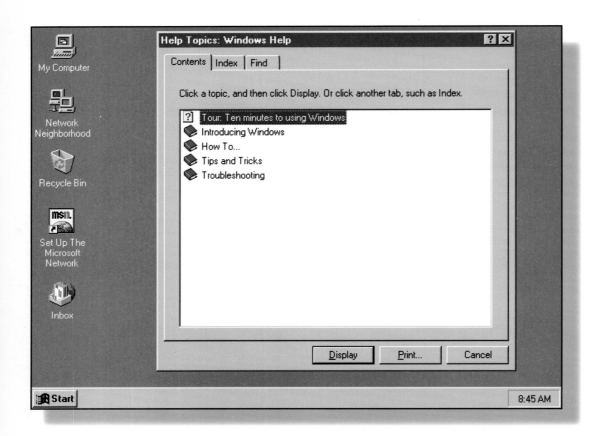

"Why would I do this?"

Whether you are a new or experienced Windows user, you will need help at some point with a procedure or task; for example, setting up a printer, finding a document, linking between applications, and so on. The newest version of Windows makes it easy and convenient to find that help. This task shows you how to start the Help feature.

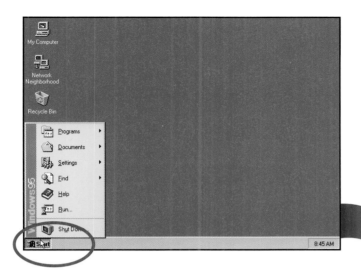

1 Click the **Start** button on the taskbar to display the Start menu.

2 From the Start menu, choose **Help**. The Help window appears. You can take a ten-minute tour of Windows 95 by clicking that option in the Contents tab.

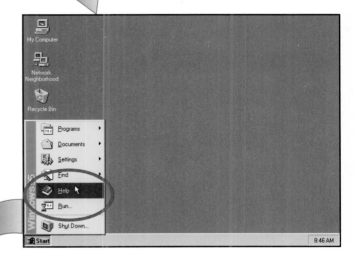

3 The Help Topics window includes three tabs (Contents, Index, and Find) from which you can choose to provide assistance. Tasks 15, 16, and 17 cover the use of these three tabs in detail; learn how to find help for any question you have. ■

TASK 15
Finding Specific Help

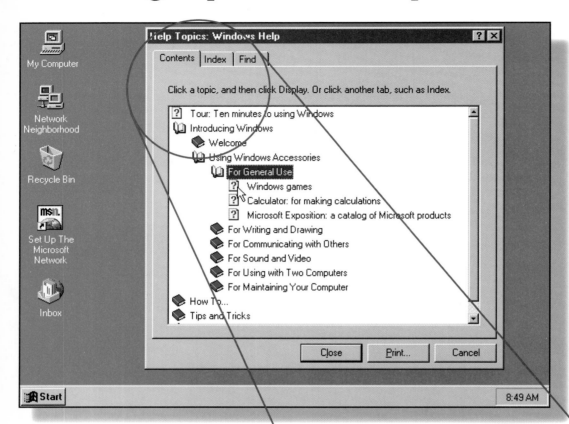

"Why would I do this?"

Use the Contents tab of the Help window to locate help for performing specific procedures, such as printing a document or installing new software. The specific topics included in the Contents tab quickly refer you to everyday tasks you perform in the program.

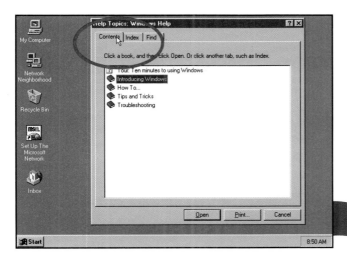

1 Start the Help program a previous task. In the Help click the **Contents** tab, i showing. The last tab you viewed is the one that appears when you open the Help window.

2 To view subtopics under any subject in the Contents tab (for example, **How To...**), click the book icon beside the topic. The topic changes to reversed video. Then click the **Open** button at the bottom of the window to open the list of subtopics. The book opens and a list of subtopics appears.

Alternatively, you can double-click the book to open it.

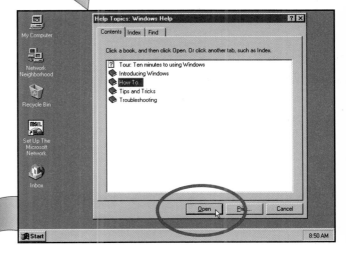

3 In the list of How To topics, double-click the topic **Print**. The book opens and a list of related topics appears.

> **NOTE** ▼
>
> You can double-click an open book icon at any time to hide the subtopics listed below that topic. Alternatively, select the open book icon and click the Close button. You also can choose any topic icon and choose the Print button to print a hard copy of the topic.

Double-click any one of the topics for more information. The Help Topics (main window) window minimizes and the topic window (secondary window) appears. When you minimize the Help Topic window, it appears as a button on the taskbar.

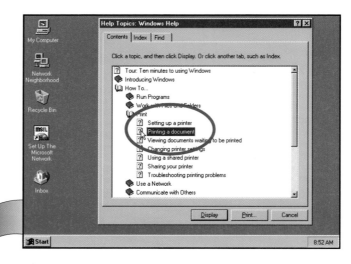

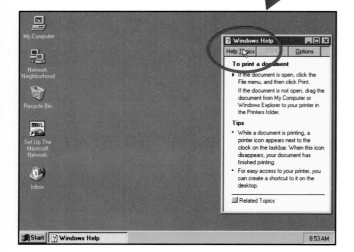

5 After viewing the Help topic, choose the **Help Topics** button to return to the Help Topic window and the Contents list. The specific topic window remains open in the background; when you choose another topic, the main Help window minimizes and the topic's procedure appears in the secondary topic window. ■

NOTE ▼

Help's secondary topic windows stay on top of all other windows (except Help's main topic window) so you can use the step-by-step procedures as you work. If you close the secondary menu, you close Help, thus removing the icon from the taskbar; minimize the secondary window if you want to use Help again later.

Locating a Topic

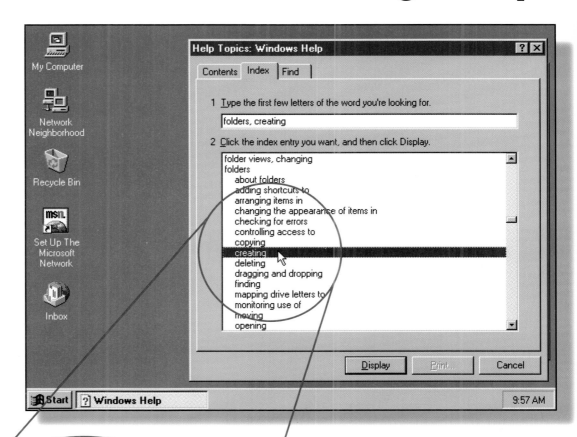

"Why would I do this?"

If you want to find help on a topic, such as sorting files by size or editing text, use the Index tab in the Help Topics window. Topics listed in the index are in alphabetical order; additionally, there are many more topics listed in the Index than in the Contents tab of the Help Topics window. This task illustrates how to use the Index in the Help Topics window.

1 Start Help, as explained in the first task of this part. In the Help Topics window, choose the **Index** tab by clicking it (if it is not already showing). A list of indexed Help topics appears.

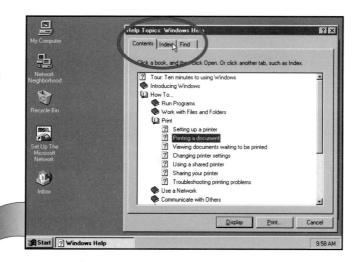

2 A blinking cursor appears in the text box at the top of the tab. Enter the name of the topic for which you want to search; in this case, type **folders**. As you type, the list jumps to the topic for which you are searching.

NOTE ▼

You can alternatively scroll through the list of topics on the Index tab; however, scrolling through the entire list takes a long time.

3 Double-click on the word **creating**, located below the list of folders subtopics. The Topics Found window appears when there is more than one topic available; choose the appropriate topic by double-clicking that topic. Otherwise, the secondary topic window appears. If the Topics Found window appears, choose the appropriate topic by double-clicking it; the secondary topic window appears, displaying a step-by-step list of how to create a folder. ■

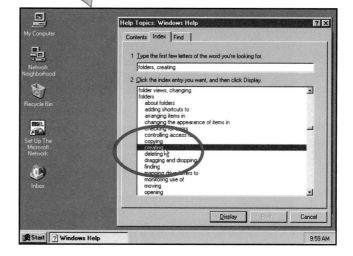

Using the Find Feature

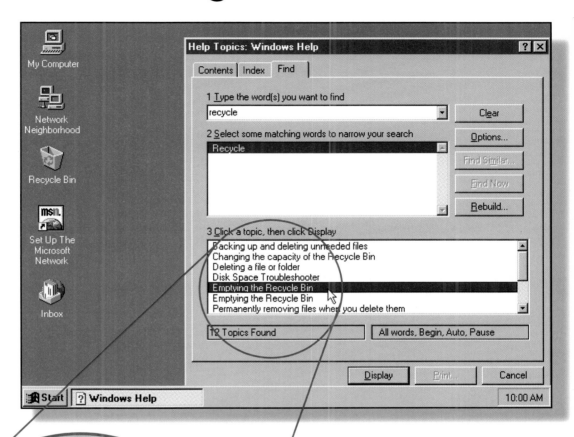

"Why would I do this?"

The Windows Help Topic called Find enables you to search for specific words within the Help topics. Before you use the Find feature, you enable Windows to compile the Find list by choosing the Find tab in the Help Topics window. You create the list only once by following the directions on-screen; thereafter, the Find list is available in the Help Topics window.

1 To view the Find list, choose the **Start** menu and the **Help** command. The Help Topics window appears. You can use Find tab to search for help on formatting disks, memory troubleshooting, saving a file, setting up a printer, and a multitude of other procedures in Windows.

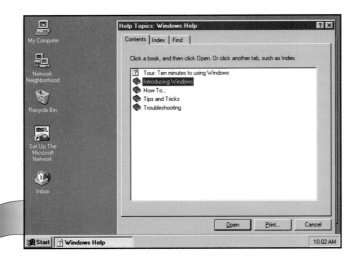

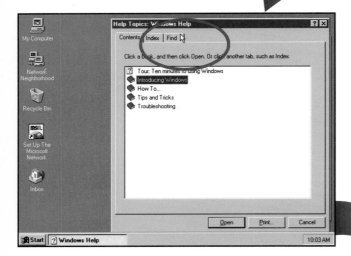

2 Choose the **Find** tab. If you have not used the Find tab before, Windows prompts you to set up the Find list. Follow the directions on-screen; it may take a few minutes to index all of the Help topics. When Windows finishes, the Find tab displays again.

3 Enter the word or words you want to find in the **1 Type the word(s)** text box, such as **recycle**. As you type, Windows jumps to a matching word or words in the second area (2 Select some matching words to narrow your search) and in the third area (3 Click a topic). Click the topic you want in the bottom list box—for example, **Emptying the Recycle Bin**—and click the **Display** button. The Help Topic secondary window appears with directions.

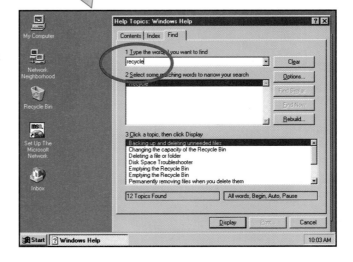

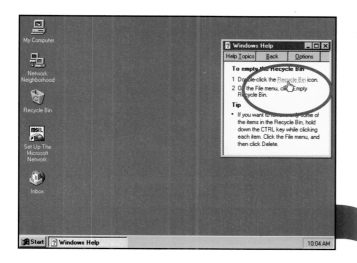

4 To read the definition of any underlined word or words in a Help window, position the mouse pointer over the word; the pointer changes to a hand. Click the mouse and a definition appears.

NOTE ▼

There are two Emptying the Re-cycle Bin Help topics: the first tells you how to empty the bin and the second offers information about viewing the contents of the bin and freeing disk space.

5 Click anywhere to close the definition box. Often secondary Help boxes contain a related subjects button at the end of the text; click on the button to find more help on the topic. Choose **Help Topics** to return to the Find tab.

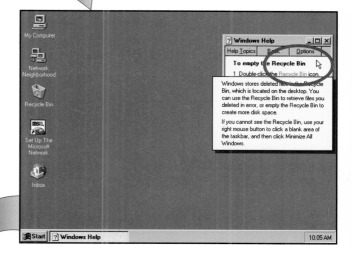

6 To close the Help Topics window, choose **Cancel**. The secondary Help window remains open; if you want to close the secondary box, click the **Close** button (**X**). ∎

Adding Notes
to a Help Topic

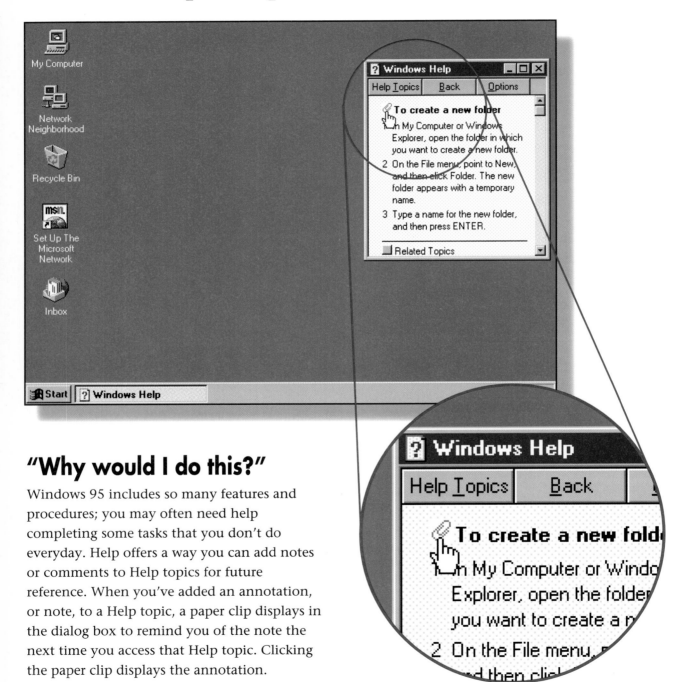

"Why would I do this?"

Windows 95 includes so many features and
procedures; you may often need help
completing some tasks that you don't do
everyday. Help offers a way you can add notes
or comments to Help topics for future
reference. When you've added an annotation,
or note, to a Help topic, a paper clip displays in
the dialog box to remind you of the note the
next time you access that Help topic. Clicking
the paper clip displays the annotation.

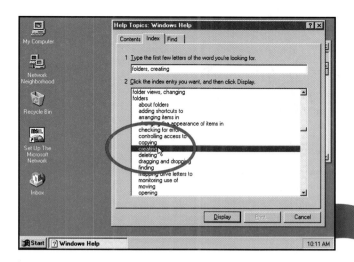

1 Open the Help window and choose the **Index** tab. In the first text box, type **folders**. Double-click on **creating**. The Topics Found window appears; from the list of topics, choose **Creating a Folder** and choose **Display**. The secondary Help window appears.

2 In the secondary Help window, click the **Options** button to display the Options menu; choose **Annotate**. Notice with this menu, you can also choose to print the topic, change the font size, copy the topic, and change system colors.

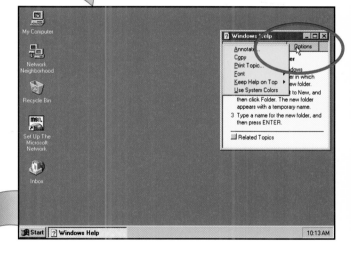

3 Enter the text in the Current Annotation text box and choose **Save**. A small paper clip appears beside the subject in the secondary Help window. To view or edit the annotation, double-click the paper clip. ■

Printing Help

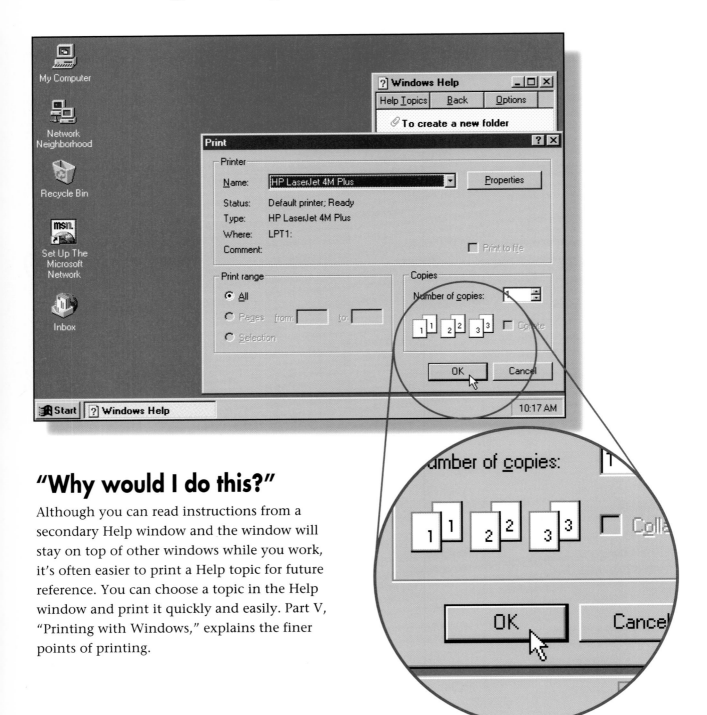

"Why would I do this?"

Although you can read instructions from a secondary Help window and the window will stay on top of other windows while you work, it's often easier to print a Help topic for future reference. You can choose a topic in the Help window and print it quickly and easily. Part V, "Printing with Windows," explains the finer points of printing.

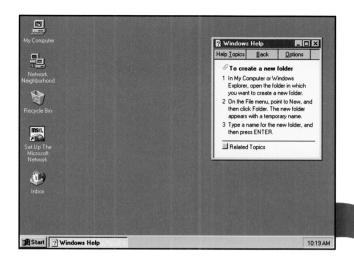

1 Display the secondary Help topics window by selecting a topic in the Index, Find, or Contents tab of the Help window.

2 In the secondary Help topics window, choose the **Options** button, and then select **Print Topic** from the menu. The Print dialog box appears. Notice the ellipsis after the menu command means a dialog box containing related options will appear.

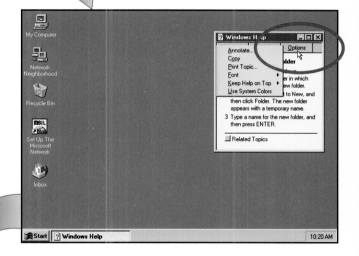

3 Choose the printer, number of copies, and print range. Choose **OK** in the Print dialog box to print the Help topic. ■

TASK 20
Using Context-Sensitive Help

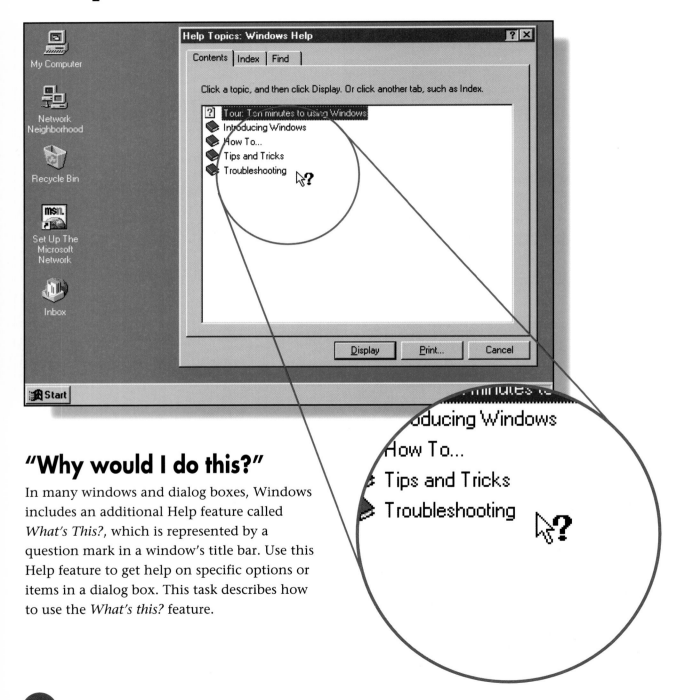

"Why would I do this?"

In many windows and dialog boxes, Windows includes an additional Help feature called *What's This?*, which is represented by a question mark in a window's title bar. Use this Help feature to get help on specific options or items in a dialog box. This task describes how to use the *What's this?* feature.

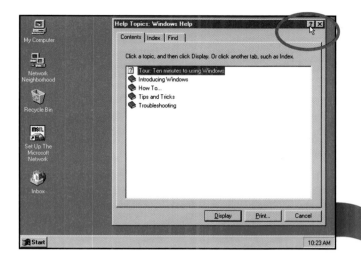

1 To use the context-sensitive *What's This?* feature, click the question mark (**?**) button in the title bar of a window or dialog box. For example, click the question mark button in the Help Topics main window. The mouse pointer changes to a pointer connected to a large question mark.

NOTE ▼

If a dialog box does not contain the What's This? question mark, try pressing the F1 button for help.

2 Move the pointer to any part of the dialog box about which you have a question. Click the left mouse button and a box appears with an explanation or definition.

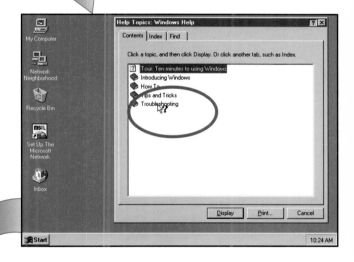

3 After reading the explanation, click the mouse anywhere within the Help box to close the context-sensitive box. Close the Help Topics window by clicking the **Close** button (**X**) in the title bar. ■

PART III

Controlling Applications

One advantage of using Windows is the enormous quantity of Windows applications available. Various companies produce word processing, database, spreadsheet, drawing, and other programs you can use in Windows. Such a variety of applications provides you with the tools you need to perform your everyday tasks. In addition to Windows applications, you can also use DOS applications in Windows.

You install all applications made for Windows in the same way: with a command line. The command line, which is found in the application's reference material, includes the drive and file name that installs the Windows application. The drive is a floppy or CD-ROM drive—A:, B:, D:, or other such designation. The specified file is an *executable file* (a file that executes a setup of the application).

The executable file, *install.exe* or *setup.exe* for example, is a program that installs files from the floppy disk or CD-ROM to your hard disk. The files it installs are the files that start and operate the new application you are introducing to Windows. Executable files are identified in Windows as an "Application" type file; common extensions for executable files are EXE, PIF, COM, and BAT.

You use the Windows Run dialog box to install new applications. "Run," in this case, means to run or operate the setup program that installs the application to your hard disk. You enter the correct drive and file name, and Windows begins the installation. During the installation, dialog boxes may appear that ask for your name, company name, or various other information.

You can also use the Run dialog box to start an application that is already installed to the computer. By entering the program's executable file name, you can run an application in Windows.

In most cases, you will install a file by entering the drive and the file name specified in the application's instructions; however, sometimes you may need to search for a specific file to install. Many application installation disks include more than one application, and you may want to install only one. Included in the Run dialog box is a command button—Browse—that enables you to view files in any drive and any directory on your computer. You can search for program files and select the one you want to run or install.

Finally, you can install DOS programs using the MS-DOS prompt from Windows. At the DOS prompt, enter the command line specified in the DOS application's documentation, and the program installs. You can then access and use the DOS program at any time through the MS-DOS prompt, which is found in the Programs list in the Start menu.

The biggest advantage of using Windows is the control it gives you over your applications. In Windows 95, you can operate both Windows and DOS applications easily and efficiently.

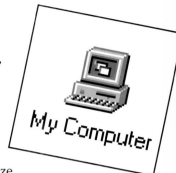

Windows applications are easy to open and use. Using the Start menu, you simply select the application from the Programs list and it opens. Additionally, you can create shortcuts representing the application that you place on the desktop so you can access the application faster. Windows also includes a method of starting an application at the same time you start the Windows program to save you time.

Each open application is contained within its own window so you can minimize, maximize, resize, move, and rearrange application windows on the desktop. Additionally, taskbar buttons represent minimized applications for quick and easy access of the program and for smooth switching between the open programs.

Windows comes with several accessory programs (a word processor, paint program, calendar, calculator, and so on) that you can open and use while working in Windows. Additional Windows applications are easily installed, as well. Any additional applications behave the same as Windows accessories; for example, you open, close, manipulate the windows, and so on, the same in WordPro or Microsoft Word as you would in the accessory WordPad.

Finally, you can even open and use DOS programs within Windows—for example, WordPerfect for DOS or Lotus 1-2-3 for DOS. It is important to realize that opening and using large files from DOS programs within Windows may take extra RAM to work efficiently. *RAM (random-access memory)* is the memory your computer uses to run programs, switch between applications, modify files, and generally carry out procedures as you work.

Less RAM causes your system to slow screen redraw, delay file commands such as saving and printing, take longer to access files, and so on. These processes may take even longer when using DOS programs within Windows. Windows recommends 4M to 8M RAM, with 8M as preferred for using DOS programs within Windows. In general, the more RAM you have, the more efficiently your computer works.

This part illustrates how to install, open, and close applications; add new Windows programs; and use the MS-DOS Prompt to open and use DOS applications in Windows.

Installing Windows Applications

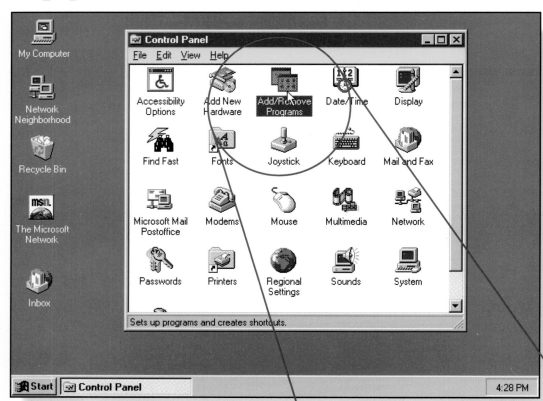

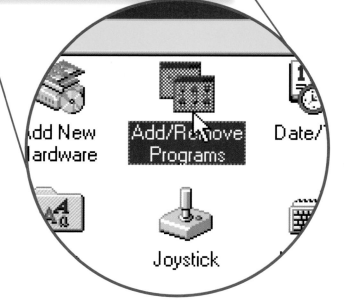

"Why would I do this?"

To make the most of Windows power, you install and use the applications you need to perform your work. You can install word processing, database, spreadsheet, or any other Windows programs to Windows 95 using the Add/Remove Programs Properties dialog box and the application's installation disks.

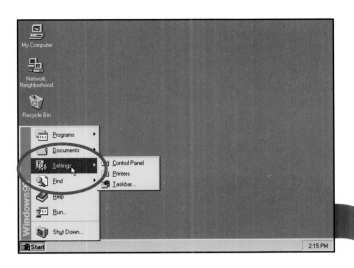

1 Insert the first installation or setup disk in your A or B floppy drive. Open the **Start** menu and choose the **Settings** command. From the secondary menu, choose the **Control Panel**. The Control Panel window appears.

2 In the Control Panel, double-click the **Add/Remove Programs** icon. Alternatively, select the **Add/Remove Programs** icon and choose **File**, **Open**. The Add/Remove Programs Properties dialog box appears.

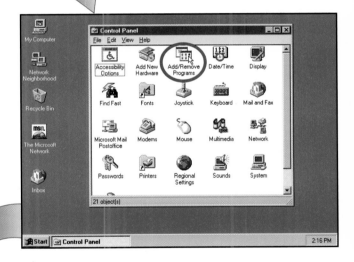

3 In the Install/Uninstall tab, click the **Install** button. The Install Program From Floppy Disk or CD-ROM dialog box appears.

4 Read the instructions, insert the application's first disk or the CD if you haven't already, and choose **Next.**

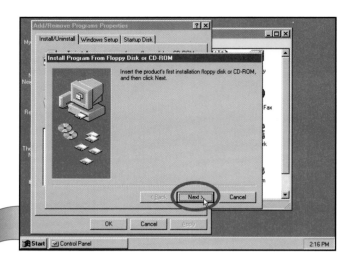

5 Windows finds the file needed to install the program and displays it in the Run Installation Program window. You can choose **Finish** to continue with the installation. You can, alternatively, choose the **Browse** command button to look at the disk and choose a different setup or installation file. Choose **Finish** and Windows installs the program. Answer any questions, change disks, and generally follow the instructions on-screen. ■

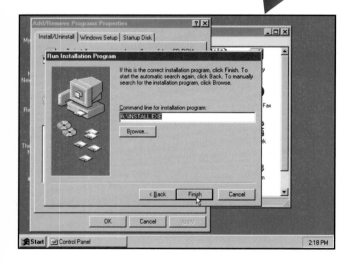

Installing DOS Applications

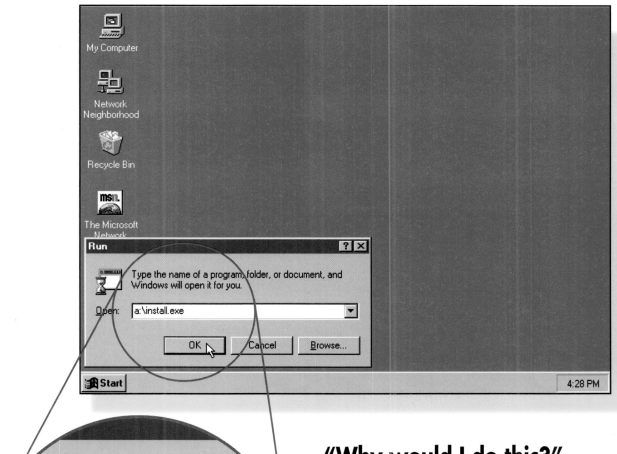

"Why would I do this?"

Many people are more familiar with some DOS applications than their Windows equivalents and would, therefore, prefer to work in the DOS applications. Windows enables you to install DOS applications, such as games, word processors, and so on, using the Run command. You also can open and use the DOS applications in Windows, as explained in later tasks.

1 Open the **Start** menu and choose the **Run** command. The Run dialog box appears. The Run command enables you to start programs and to install programs.

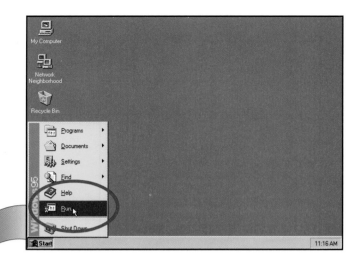

2 In the **Open** text box, enter the disk drive and the command line to install or setup the program. Skip to step 5. If you do not know the command line, enter the drive letter and a colon (**a:**) and then click the **Browse** button.

3 The Browse dialog box appears and lists the files on the disk or CD. Select the file titled **Install** or **Setup** and choose **Open**.

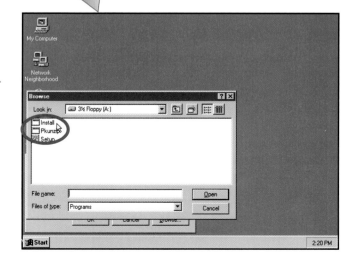

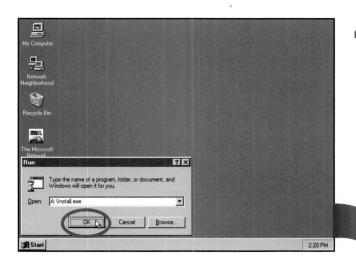

4 The Browse dialog box closes, and Windows returns to the Run dialog box. The command line lists the drive and the install or setup command. Choose **OK** to install the program.

5 Depending on the program you install, Windows may return to the desktop or return to the MS-DOS Prompt window. You can open the application in the MS-DOS window; see Tasks 28 and 29 for more information. To close the MS-DOS Prompt window, type **exit** and press **Enter**. ■

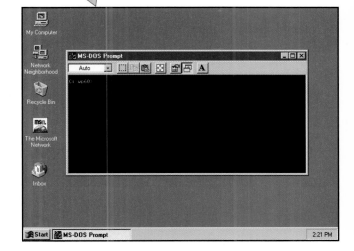

73

Starting an Application with the Start Menu

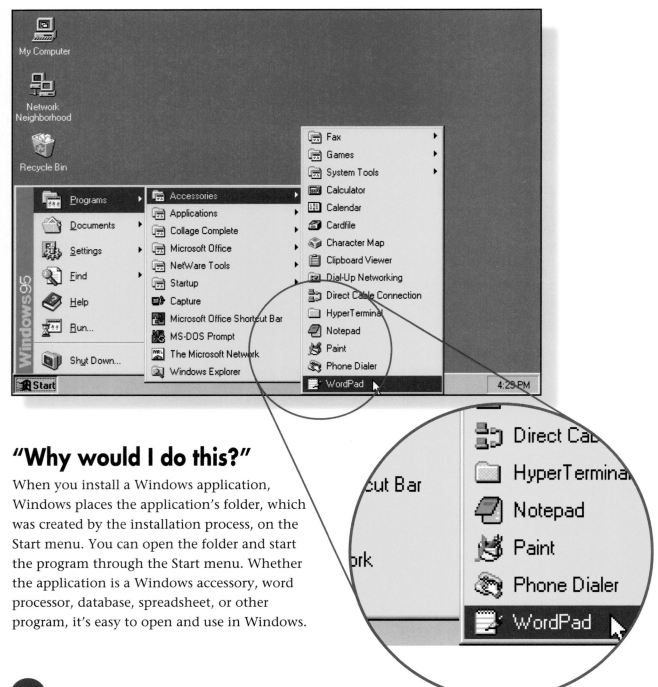

"Why would I do this?"

When you install a Windows application, Windows places the application's folder, which was created by the installation process, on the Start menu. You can open the folder and start the program through the Start menu. Whether the application is a Windows accessory, word processor, database, spreadsheet, or other program, it's easy to open and use in Windows.

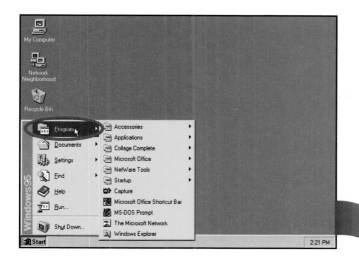

1 Open the **Start** menu and choose the **Programs** command. The Programs menu appears.

2 On the **Programs** menu, select the program group that contains the application you want to start. The folder's contents appear on a secondary menu.

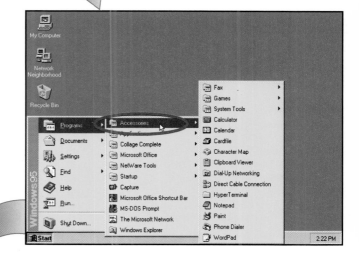

3 Click on the application you want to start. The application opens in its own window.

Starting an Application When You Start Windows

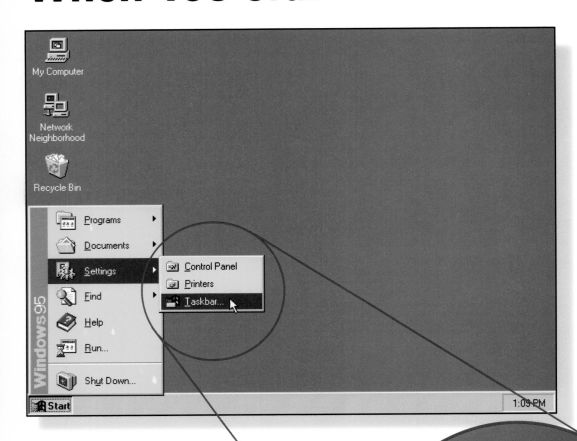

"Why would I do this?"

Windows enables you to start one or more programs with Windows when you turn your computer on. Applications you might want to open automatically are those you use every day or any you use the first thing each day. Opening applications with Windows is a shortcut to opening the program after Windows loads.

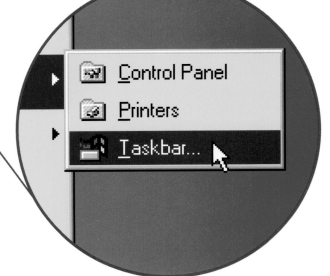

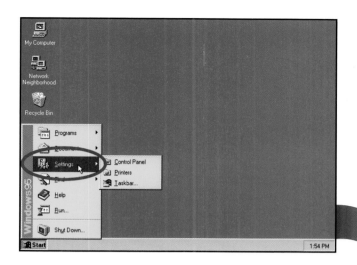

1 Open the **Start** menu. When the Start menu appears, move the mouse to **Settings**, and a secondary menu appears. Click **Taskbar** to open the Taskbar Properties window.

2 Click the **Start Menu Programs** tab. Click **Add**, and the Create Shortcut dialog box appears.

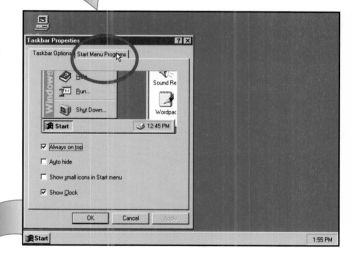

3 Click the **Browse** button to open the Browse window. Click the drop-down arrow to display the **Look In** drop-down list, and then choose the folder that contains the program you want to open when Windows starts. The list box displays the contents of the folder.

4 Double-click the program you want to start with Windows, in this case, WordPad. The Browse dialog box closes and the command line for the program you selected appears in the Create Shortcut dialog box.

> **NOTE** ▼
>
> WordPad's command line is in the PROGRAMS/ACCESSORIES folder.

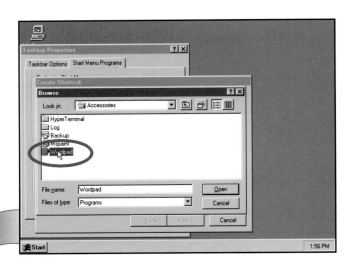

5 Click the **Next** button to display the Select Program Folder dialog box. Then double-click the **StartUp** folder to display the Select a Title for the Program dialog box.

> **WHY WORRY?**
>
> To remove an icon from the Startup window, choose the Remove button in the Start Menu Programs tab of the Taskbar Properties dialog box. Then choose the item you want to remove from the menu and click the Remove button. Close the Remove Shortcuts/Folders dialog box, and then choose OK.

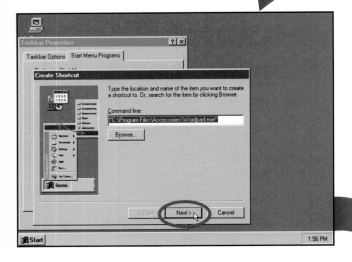

6 Enter a title to place in the StartUp menu or use the one Windows suggests. Click **Finish**. If Windows asks you to choose an icon, click one and then click **Finish**. Choose **OK** in the Taskbar Properties dialog box to close it and return to the desktop. ■

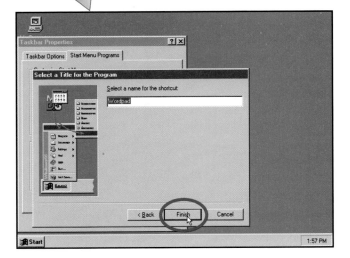

Starting an Application from a File

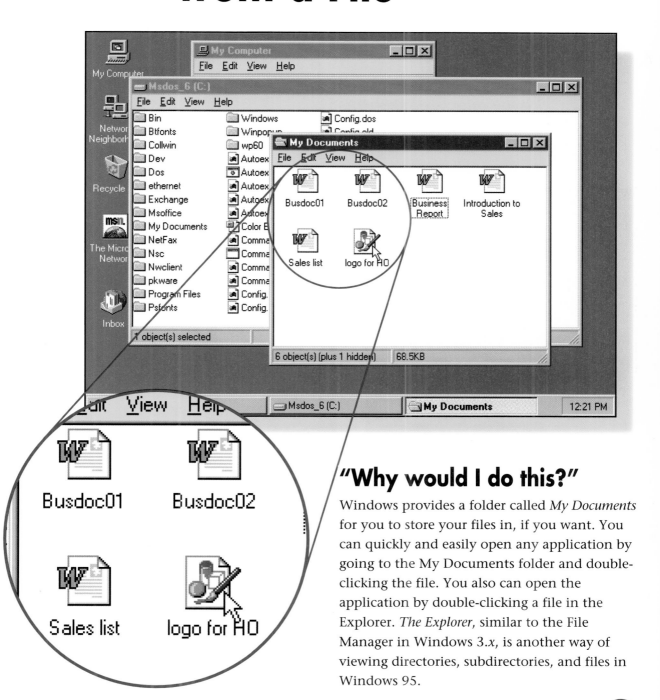

"Why would I do this?"

Windows provides a folder called *My Documents* for you to store your files in, if you want. You can quickly and easily open any application by going to the My Documents folder and double-clicking the file. You also can open the application by double-clicking a file in the Explorer. *The Explorer*, similar to the File Manager in Windows 3.*x*, is another way of viewing directories, subdirectories, and files in Windows 95.

1 Open the **My Computer** window and then open your hard drive window.

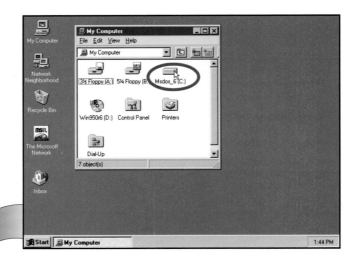

2 Open the **My Documents** folder to display all documents you've saved there.

> **NOTE** ▼
>
> You also can create new documents in the My Document window. Choose File, New and select an application to use to create the document. The applications listed are programs you've added to your Windows 95 setup, such as Word, Excel, and so on. The Windows Accessories (WordPad, MS Paint, and so on) are not listed in this menu although you can save documents created in the Accessories applications in My Document.

3 Double-click any file created in an application on your machine. The application opens with the file ready to work on or print.

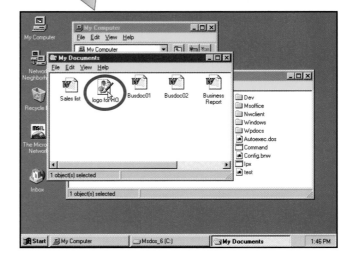

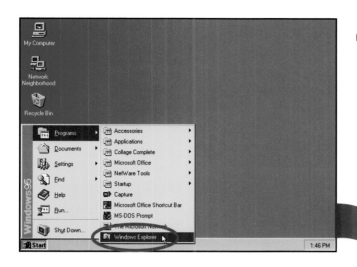

4 To open the Explorer, open the **Start** menu and choose **Programs**. From the secondary menu, choose **Windows Explorer**.

5 In the left side of the Explorer window, select the folder containing the saved file you want to open. A list of subdirectories, or folders, appears on the right side of the window. Depending on the folder you select on the left side of the window, the right side may also list files contained in the folder.

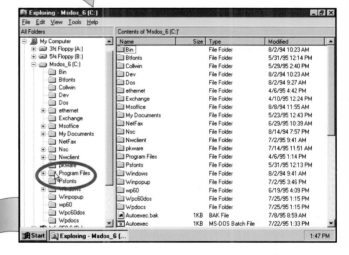

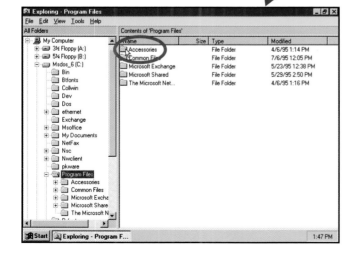

6 On the right side of the window, double-click the folder holding the saved file.

7 Double-click the file to open it within its application.

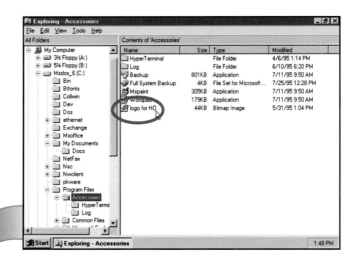

8 When you're done with the file, close the application by choosing **File**, **Exit**. Windows closes the application and returns to the Windows Explorer.

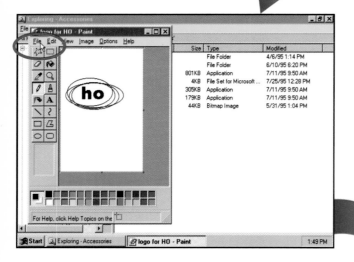

9 To close the Windows Explorer, choose **File**, **Close**.

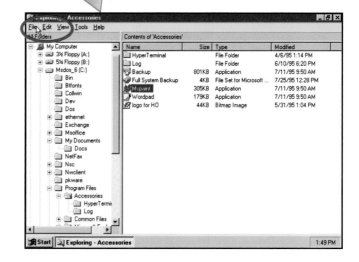

Saving Your Work

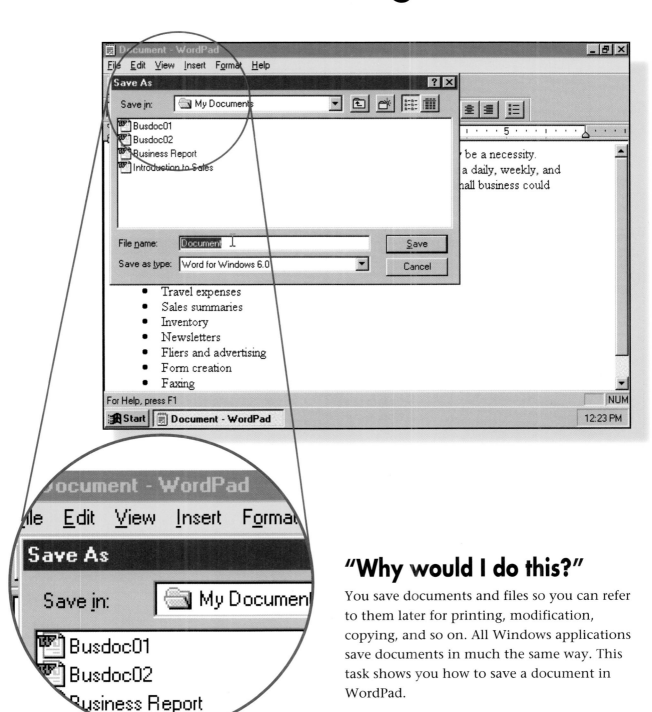

"Why would I do this?"

You save documents and files so you can refer to them later for printing, modification, copying, and so on. All Windows applications save documents in much the same way. This task shows you how to save a document in WordPad.

1 In the application, choose the **File** menu and the **Save As** command. The Save As dialog box appears.

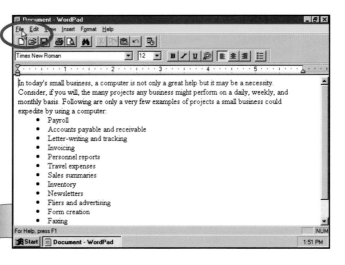

2 In the File Name text box, enter the name of the file you want to save. You can use spaces and other punctuation, along with numbers and letters, in the file name. If you save the file in the current folder, you will always be able to find it when you need to open it later for revisions or printing. If you want to save the file in the current folder, choose **Save**.

3 You can, alternatively, save the file in the My Documents folder so all of your files will be together and easy to find. To save the file in the My Documents folder, click the **Up One Level** button. The folders on the hard drive appear in the list.

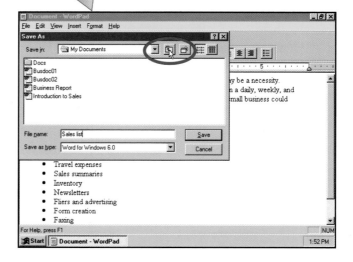

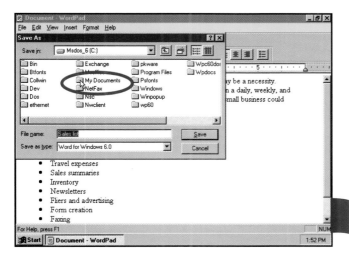

4 Double-click the **My Documents** folder.

5 The folder opens, displaying other files if you have saved files there before. Make sure the name of your file is what you want and then choose the **Save** command button. The application saves the file and returns to the document window. ■

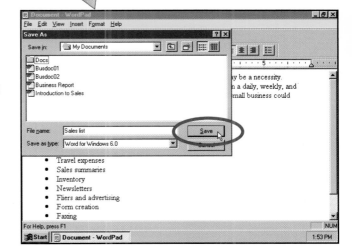

Closing an Application

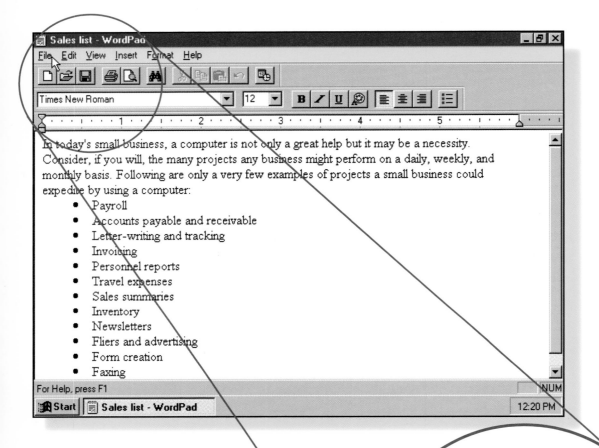

"Why would I do this?"

You can leave applications open for later use (minimize them), just as you can leave windows open. However, when you finish working in a program, you will want to close that program to free system memory. Too many open applications can tax your system's memory and slow the computer's processes, such as saving, printing, switching between applications, and so on.

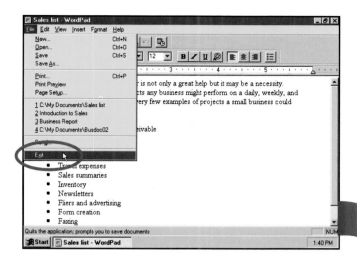

1 To close an application, open the application's **File** menu and choose the **Exit** command. Every Windows application works the same.

2 A second method of closing an application is to open the application's **Control** menu by clicking on the icon in the left corner of the title bar. From the Control menu, choose **Close**; alternatively, press **Alt+F4**.

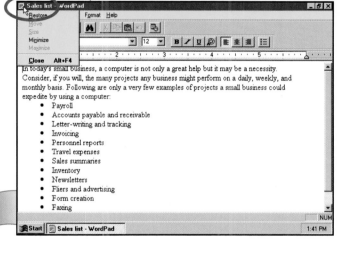

3 The final method of closing an application is to click the **Close** button (**X**) in the application's title bar. ■

NOTE

If you have not saved a file and choose to close the application, a message box appears asking if you want to save. If you do want to save, choose Yes; if not, choose No. If you want to return to the document, choose Cancel.

Using the MS-DOS Prompt

"Why would I do this?"

There will be times you want to access the DOS prompt from Windows—for example, to run a DOS application or to use DOS commands, such as MEM, SCANDISK, and so on. Windows provides a DOS prompt window you can open while working in Windows.

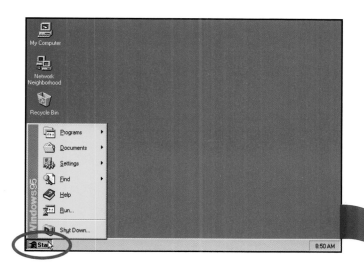

1 Open the **Start** menu. Move the mouse pointer to **Programs**, and the secondary menu appears.

2 Move the mouse pointer to **MS-DOS Prompt** and click. The DOS window appears with a blinking cursor at the DOS prompt.

> **NOTE** ▼
>
> You can use the icons at the top of the DOS window to mark, copy, paste, enlarge to full screen, set the background, and set the font of the DOS window.

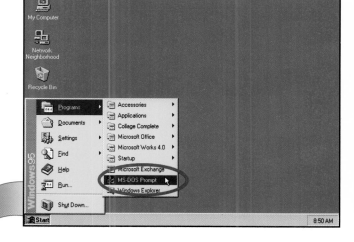

3 Type **cd** and press **Enter** to change to the root directory. Run any program by typing the appropriate DOS command.

> **NOTE** ▼
>
> Your mouse will only work in the DOS Prompt window if you have loaded a mouse driver to DOS. You can refer to the documentation that came with your mouse for instructions.

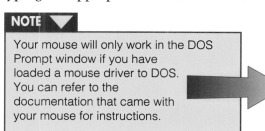

89

4 When you are ready to work with Windows again, click the **Minimize** button on the DOS window. The window reduces to a button on the taskbar, and you can work in other windows until you need the DOS window again. Click the **MS-DOS Prompt** button on the Windows Taskbar at any time to open the DOS window.

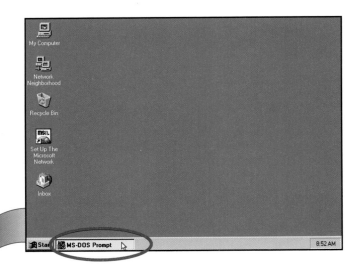

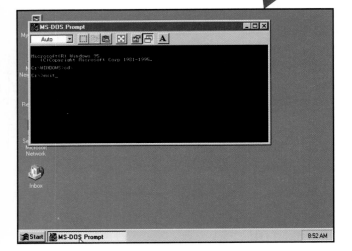

5 Type **exit** at the DOS prompt and press **Enter** to close the MS-DOS Prompt window. ■

WHY WORRY?

Press Alt+Enter to enlarge the DOS window to full screen; when you finish, press Alt+Enter again to restore the DOS window to its original size.

DOS Window Toolbar Icons

Icon	Purpose
Auto	Changes the size of the screen and, therefore, the font on-screen. For best results, choose a font with TT (TrueType) in front of it. TrueType fonts print exactly what you see on-screen.
	Mark text or a graphic to be copied by drawing a rectangle around it with the mouse.
	Click to copy any items you have marked with the Mark icon.
	Position the insertion point on the screen, and click the Paste icon to paste the copied items.
	Enlarge the MS-DOS Prompt window to fill the entire screen. Press Alt+Enter to restore the window's original size.
	Click to display the MS-DOS Prompt Properties dialog box in which you can choose advanced options for formatting the DOS window.
	Defines whether the program enables background activity, such as background printing. When performing activities in the background, some computers will become lethargic because the computer is trying to do two or more things at one time.
A	Click to display the MS-DOS Prompt Properties dialog box. Change the font types to display only bitmap or only TrueType instead of the default, which is displaying both types of fonts.

Using DOS Applications in Windows

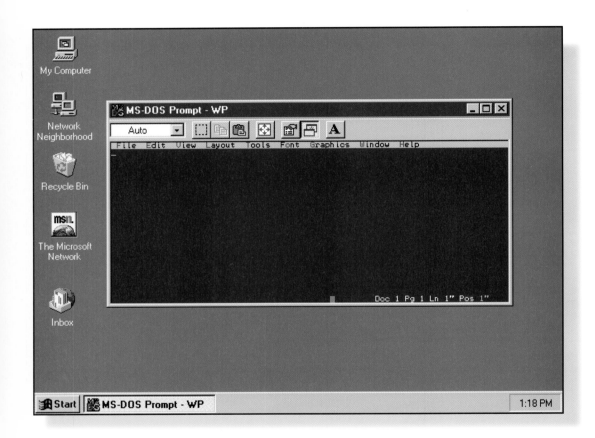

"Why would I do this?"

Run a DOS application, such as WordPerfect or Lotus 1-2-3, in Windows so you can also work in Windows at the same time. By minimizing the DOS window, you can then open and use other Windows or DOS programs and switch to the program you need quickly and easily. This task shows you how to use a DOS application in Windows.

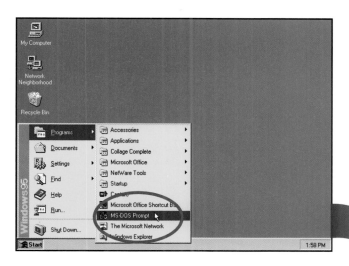

1 Open the **Start** menu; choose **Programs**. A secondary menu appears. Choose the **MS-DOS Prompt** and the DOS window appears.

2 Type **cd** and press **Enter** to move to the root directory, or change to the directory holding the DOS application (for example, **cd\wp60** for WordPerfect for DOS 6.0) and press **Enter**. Then enter the name of the program's executable file at the DOS prompt and press **Enter**; for example, **wp** starts the WordPerfect program. The DOS application appears in the DOS window and you can continue your work.

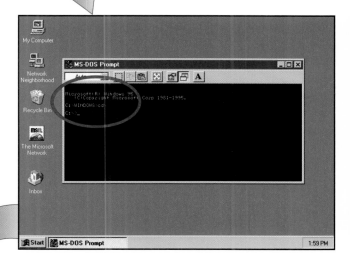

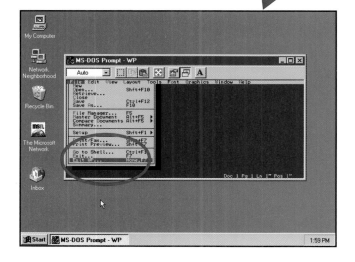

3 When you finish with the DOS application, exit the program as you normally would (choose **File**, **Exit**, for example) and Windows returns to the DOS prompt. Type **exit** and press **Enter** to close the DOS window. ■

NOTE ▼

If the application does not start from the root directory when you enter the name of the program's executable file, then you must change to the program's directory.

Accessing Application Folders

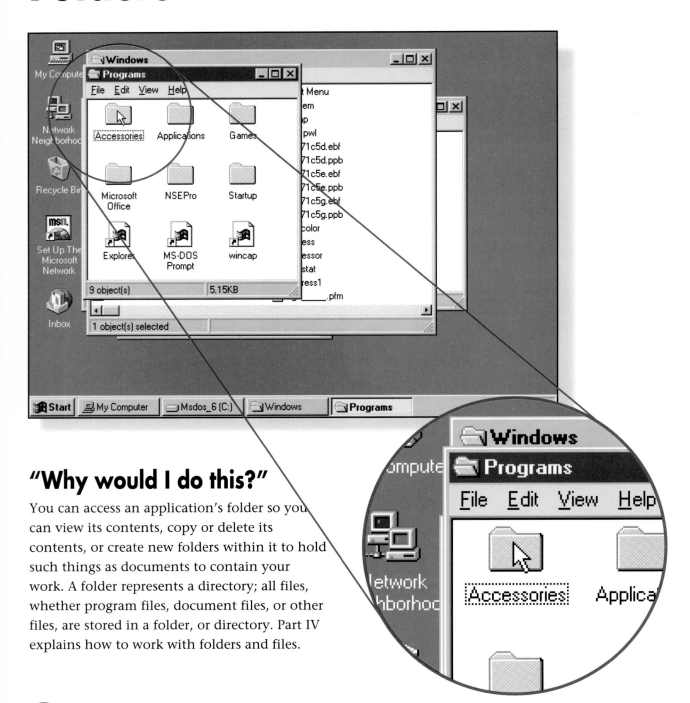

"Why would I do this?"

You can access an application's folder so you
can view its contents, copy or delete its
contents, or create new folders within it to hold
such things as documents to contain your
work. A folder represents a directory; all files,
whether program files, document files, or other
files, are stored in a folder, or directory. Part IV
explains how to work with folders and files.

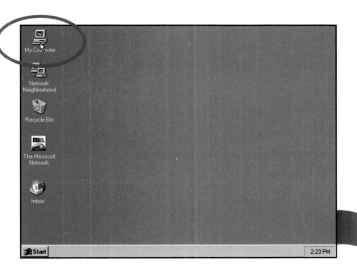

1 Open the My Computer window by double-clicking the **My Computer** icon. The My Computer window contains two folders, or directories: the Control Panel and Printers.

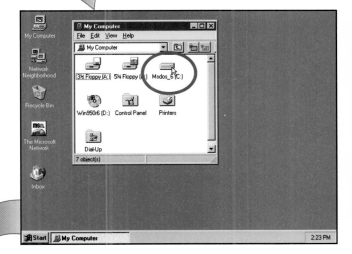

2 Open the hard drive window by double-clicking the icon representing your hard drive, usually **C**. The hard drive window lists all folders and a few files. Each folder represents directories holding related files.

3 Open the window for the Windows folder by double-clicking the **Windows** folder icon. The Windows folder contains only those programs and files used in Windows.

4 Open the Programs window by double-clicking the **Programs** folder icon in the Windows window. The Programs folder contains the Accessories, Application, Games, and Startup folders (as well as others) you see when you open the Programs menu from the Start menu.

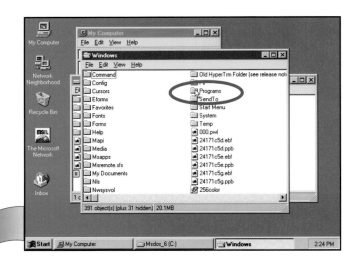

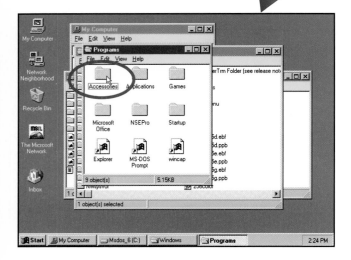

5 View an application folder's contents by double-clicking its icon in the Programs window. For example, double-click the **Accessories** icon to view the contents of the Accessories folder. You can use the menus of the application's window to create new folders, copy and paste an application icon elsewhere, and so on. When you finish in the application's window, click the **Close** button (**X**) in the title bar to close the window. Continue clicking the **Close** button in each window until you close all windows, if you prefer the windows closed. ■

> **NOTE** ▼
>
> For easier access the next time you need to open an application folder, you can create a shortcut to the folder, as explained in the following task.

Adding and Using Shortcuts

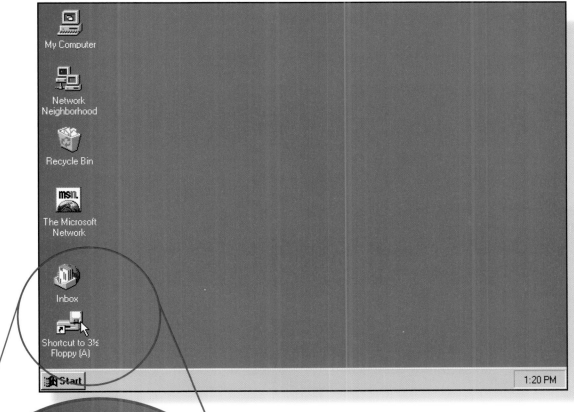

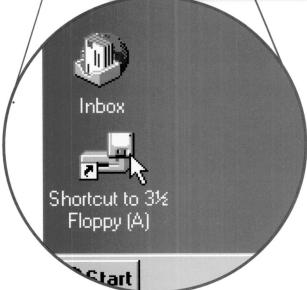

"Why would I do this?"

You can create shortcuts to quickly open programs, folders, and documents and place the shortcuts on the desktop. Click a shortcut instead of opening menus and folders to go to an item you often use.

1 Open the My Computer window by double-clicking the **My Computer** icon.

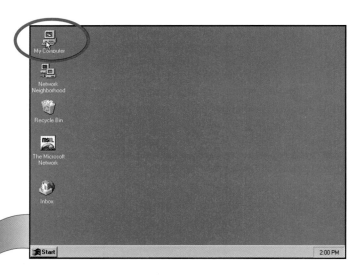

2 Select the **A** drive by clicking the mouse once on the icon. The icon changes color to indicate it is selected.

WHY WORRY?

If you do not have an A drive or a floppy disk to use in this exercise, choose the Control Panel folder instead of the drive icon. The exercise works exactly the same.

3 Open the **File** menu by clicking it. The menu displays a list of commands. Choose the **Create Shortcut** command.

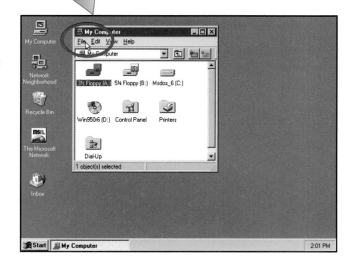

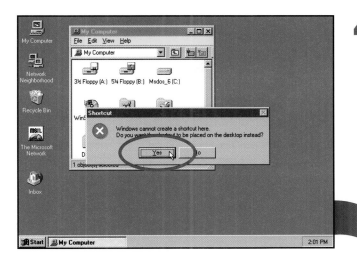

4 Insert any disk into the floppy drive. A Shortcut message appears asking if you want the shortcut placed on the desktop. Choose **Yes**. The shortcut appears on the desktop. It looks just like the item's icon with an arrow pointing to it.

5 Close the My Computer window by clicking the **Close** button (**X**) in the title bar.

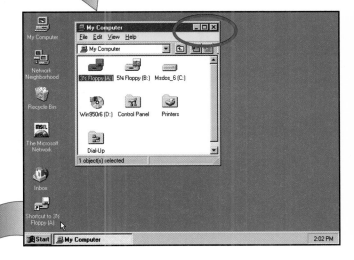

6 To quickly access drive A, make sure you have inserted a disk in drive A and then double-click the shortcut icon on the desktop. The Floppy Drive window opens, displaying the items contained on the floppy disk. ▦

NOTE ▼

Close the floppy drive window as you would any other: double-click the Control-menu box, press Alt+F4, or click the Close button in the title bar.

99

Deleting Shortcuts

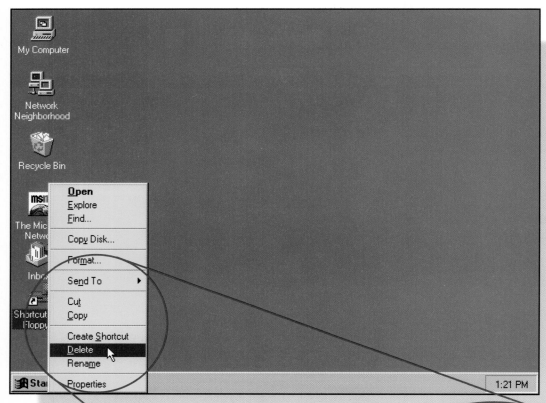

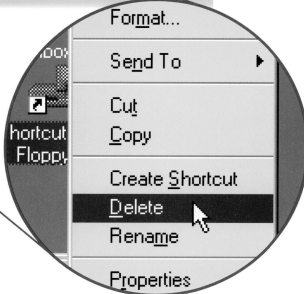

"Why would I do this?"

You use shortcuts to quickly get you to the drive, document, application, or folder you use most often; as time passes many of those items will change, and the desktop can get cluttered. You can always create new shortcuts as new documents or folders appear, and you can delete those shortcuts you no longer use.

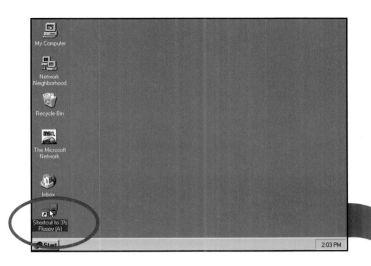

1 Select the shortcut by clicking it. The shortcut changes color.

WHY WORRY?

Deleting a shortcut does not delete the item it represents.

2 Point to the selected icon and click the right mouse button. A quick menu appears. Choose the **Delete** command. Windows displays a confirmation message.

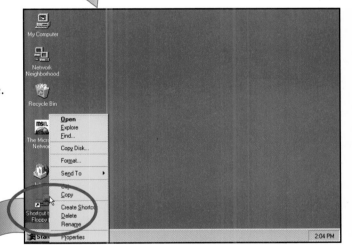

3 Choose **Yes** to delete the shortcut. Windows removes the shortcut to the Recycle Bin. To truly delete the shortcut, you must empty the bin.

4 Click the **Recycle Bin** to select it. The Bin changes colors.

> **NOTE** ▼
>
> You can restore an item you've deleted to the Recycle Bin, in case you change your mind about deleting the item completely. To restore an item, right-click the Recycle Bin to display the quick menu. Choose Open. In the Recycle Bin window, click on the item you want to restore and choose File, Restore. The item returns to its original location. Close the Recycle Bin by clicking the Close button.

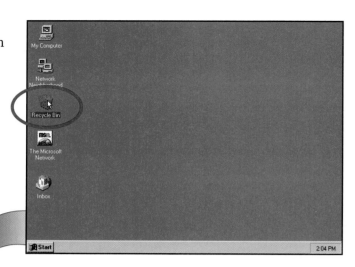

5 Click the right-mouse button to display the Recycle Bin's quick menu. Choose **Empty Recycle Bin**. Notice you also could choose **Open** to view the contents of the Recycle Bin, in case you've forgotten what you placed in it.

6 Choose **Yes** to delete the contents of the Recycle Bin. If you choose **No**, the contents remain in the bin. You can open the Bin and copy any items to another folder to keep from deleting it, if you want. ■

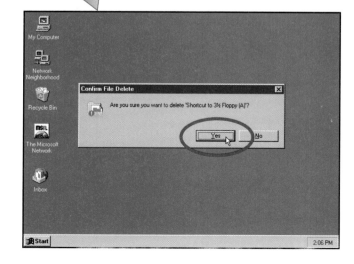

number or letter. The asterisk, on the other hand, represents more than one character in the file name. To find, for example, all files ending with an EXE extension, you enter ***.EXE**. Windows will find such examples as INSTALL.EXE, SETUP.EXE, WP.EXE, and so on. Furthermore, you can search for files of a specific type, such as application or document files. Using the Find feature enables you to quickly locate your files and folders.

Second, Windows stores your program and document files in folders that you can view in My Computer and in the Windows Explorer. Folders were, in previous versions of Windows, called directories. In Windows 95, you can create folders within folders, just as you could create subdirectories within directories. Additionally, you can store files in folders as well as copy and move files from folder to folder.

My Computer is a window containing icons representing your hard drive, floppy drives, tape and CD drives, and so on. You can open the hard drive, for example, to view the contents, select folders, add new folders, and otherwise manipulate and modify the folders in your computer. Learn to open My Computer and your hard drive in Part I.

The Explorer is the Windows 95 version of the File Manager from Windows 3.x and works similarly. Access the Explorer by opening the **Start** menu and choosing **Programs**, **Windows Explorer**. In the Explorer, you can view and select folders, add new folders, rename folders and files, and otherwise manipulate the contents just like in the My Computer window. One major difference between My Computer and the Explorer is that in the Explorer, you can view all folders in one part of the window while viewing a specific folder's contents in another part of the window, which makes copying and moving files easier. Each time you open a folder from the My Computer window, another window opens, which can tend to clutter the desktop.

Opening Folders

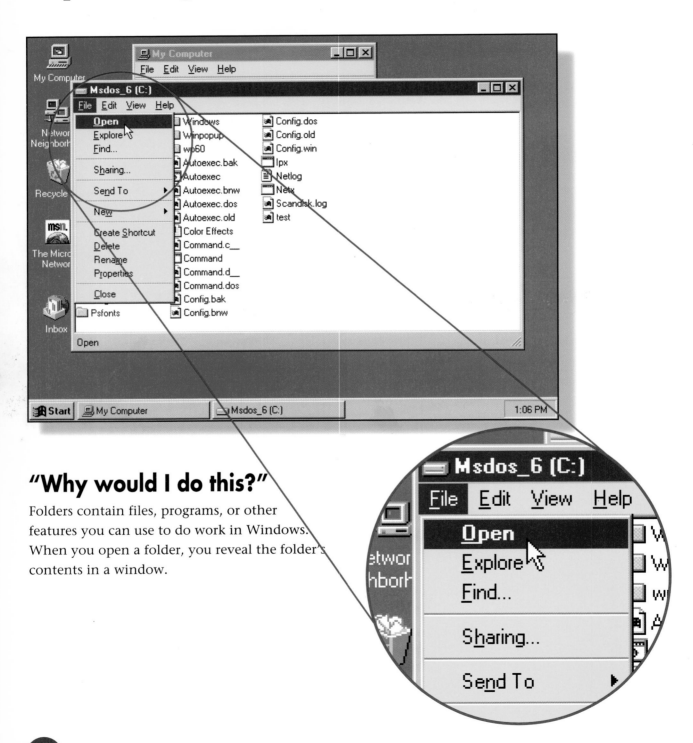

"Why would I do this?"

Folders contain files, programs, or other
features you can use to do work in Windows.
When you open a folder, you reveal the folder's
contents in a window.

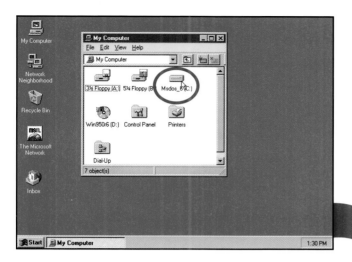

1 Double-click the **My Computer** icon on the desktop. The My Computer window opens. In the My Computer window, double-click the icon representing your hard drive. The drive window appears with icons representing folders, or directories, on your hard drive.

2 Select the Dos Folder in the drive window by clicking the folder icon once. The icon appears in a different color.

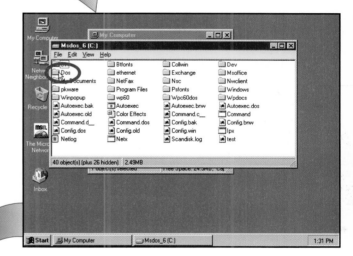

> ### NOTE ▼
> There are several types of icons in the hard drive window: file folders representing groups of files and folders, page icons representing individual files, spiral notebook icons representing WordPad files, and so on.

3 Open the **File** menu and choose the **Open** command. The Dos Folder opens in a separate window. Alternatively to steps 2 and 3, you can double-click the folder to open it. ■

> ### WHY WORRY?
> To close any folder or window, click that window's Close button (it looks like an X and is located in the right corner of the title bar).

Creating a Folder

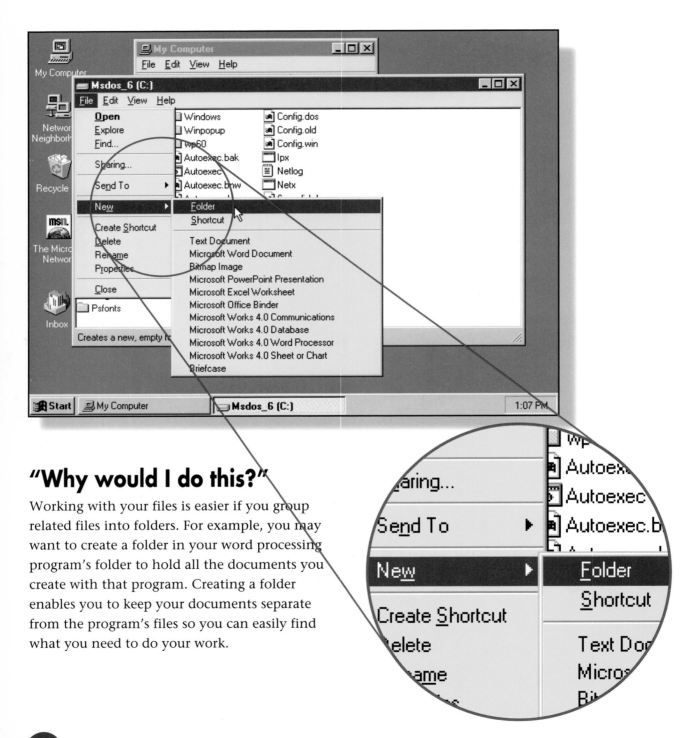

"Why would I do this?"

Working with your files is easier if you group related files into folders. For example, you may want to create a folder in your word processing program's folder to hold all the documents you create with that program. Creating a folder enables you to keep your documents separate from the program's files so you can easily find what you need to do your work.

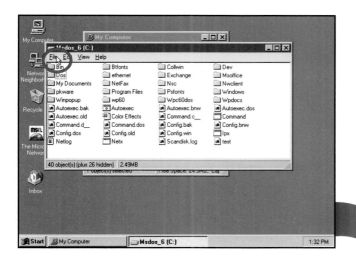

1 Open the window for the folder or disk where you want to create the new folder. For example, open the window for your hard drive. Then open the **File** menu and choose the **New** command. A secondary menu appears.

2 From the secondary menu, choose the **Folder** command. The new folder appears in the drive window.

WHY WORRY?

If you change your mind about the new folder, you can always delete it. To delete the folder, select it and press the Delete key.

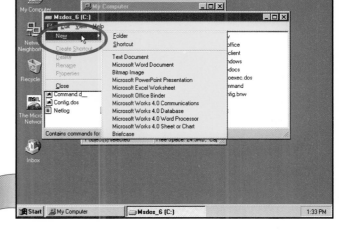

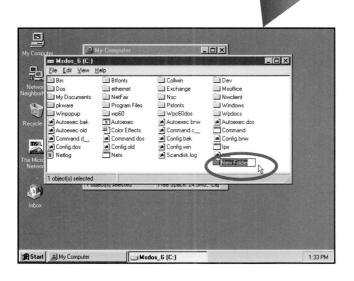

3 Click the mouse on the folder's name, **New Folder**. The mouse pointer changes to an I-beam and the name of the folder is highlighted. Enter a new name for the folder; when you type, the old name disappears. Press **Enter** when you finish typing to accept the new name. ■

Copying Folders

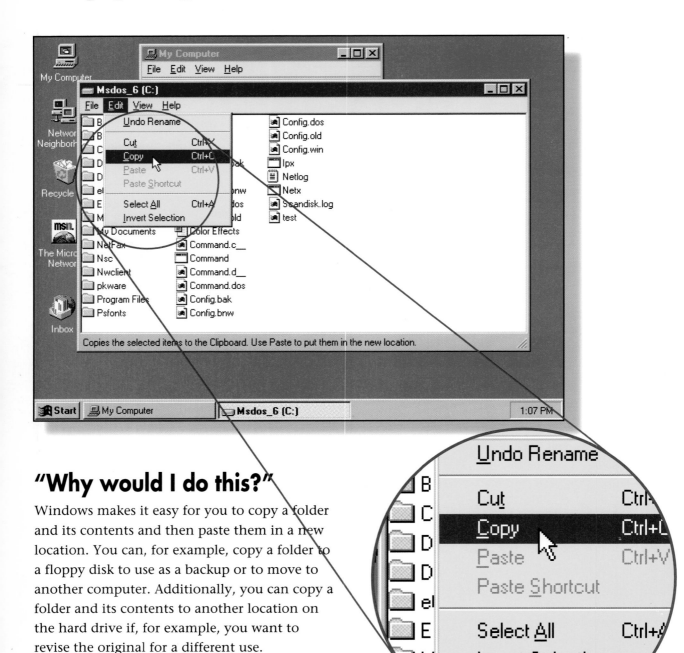

"Why would I do this?"

Windows makes it easy for you to copy a folder and its contents and then paste them in a new location. You can, for example, copy a folder to a floppy disk to use as a backup or to move to another computer. Additionally, you can copy a folder and its contents to another location on the hard drive if, for example, you want to revise the original for a different use.

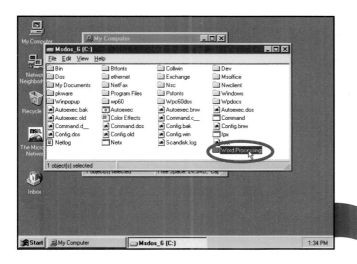

1 Insert a disk in your A or B drive. In your hard drive window, select the new folder you created in the last task.

> **NOTE** ▼
>
> To copy more than one folder at a time, hold the Ctrl key and then click each folder you want to copy. Release the Ctrl key before choosing the Copy command.

2 Open the **Edit** menu and choose the **Copy** command to copy the folder. The menu closes.

> **NOTE** ▼
>
> You can also copy a folder by first opening both the window that contains the folder (the source) and the window you want to copy the folder to (the destination). Then click the folder in the source window and drag it to the destination window.

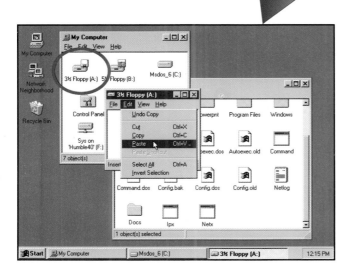

3 Double-click the drive icon for your floppy disk in the My Computer window to open it. In the floppy drive window, open the **Edit** menu and choose **Paste**. Windows copies the new folder, and its contents, to the floppy disk. As Windows copies the folder, a message box appears; when the box disappears, the copying and pasting is complete. ■

Moving Folders

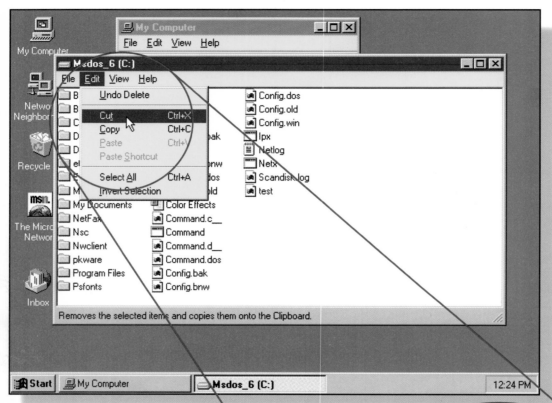

"Why would I do this?"

You can move a folder and its contents to another folder or to a disk so you can reorganize your directory structure. Suppose you wanted to move all related files and folders to the same place on your hard drive so you can find them quickly and easily, you can move those folders to one folder for better organization of your hard drive.

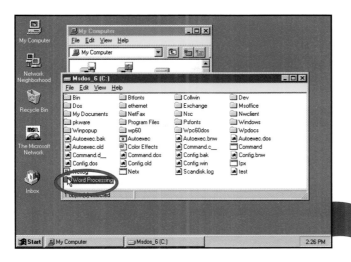

1 Select the new folder you created in Task 34.

2 Open the **Edit** menu and choose the **Cut** command to move the folder. The menu closes and only a ghost of the cut folder shows in the window. The folder is moved to the Clipboard until you're ready to paste it.

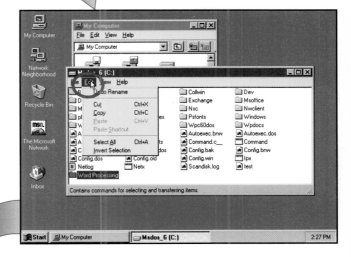

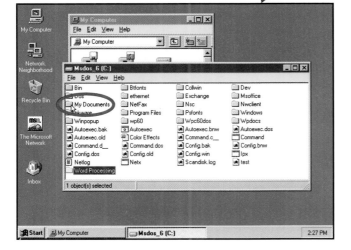

3 Double-click the **My Documents** folder in your hard drive window. In the My Documents window, open the **Edit** menu and choose **Paste**. Windows moves the folder to the floppy disk. ■

Renaming Folders

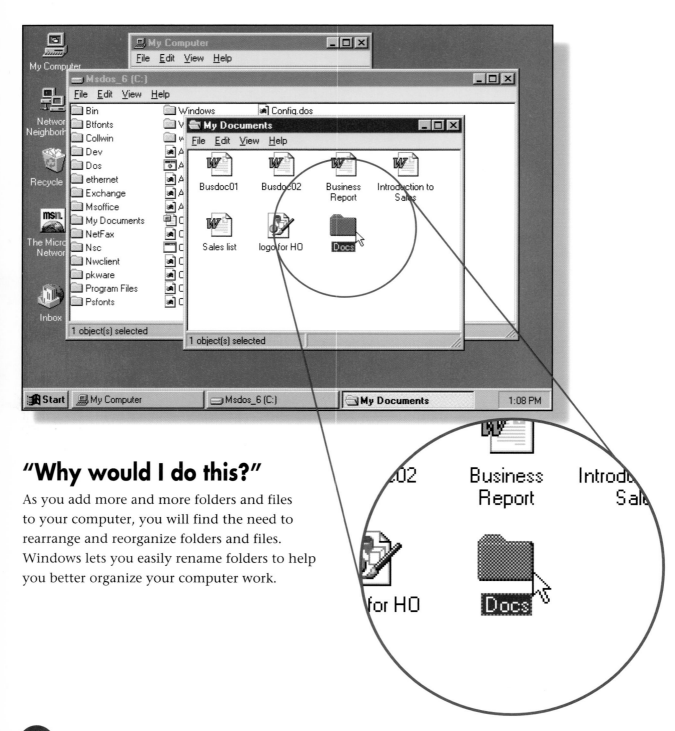

"Why would I do this?"

As you add more and more folders and files
to your computer, you will find the need to
rearrange and reorganize folders and files.
Windows lets you easily rename folders to help
you better organize your computer work.

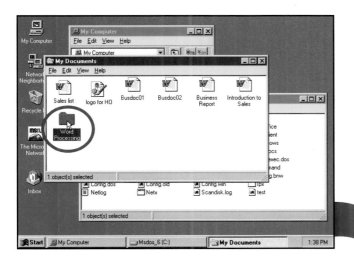

1 Click the folder once to select it; the folder changes color.

2 Click the folder's name to display the mouse I-beam and to select the folder's name.

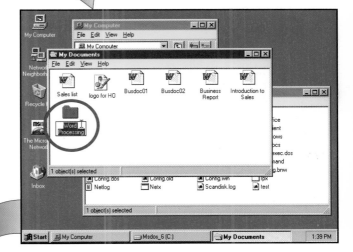

3 Enter the new name for the folder and press **Enter** to accept the name. ■

When naming or renaming folders or files, you can apply a name containing up to 255 characters, including spaces. You also can name a folder or file with letters, numbers, and other symbols on your keyboard, except the following:

\ ? : * " < > |.

TASK 38

Deleting Folders and Files

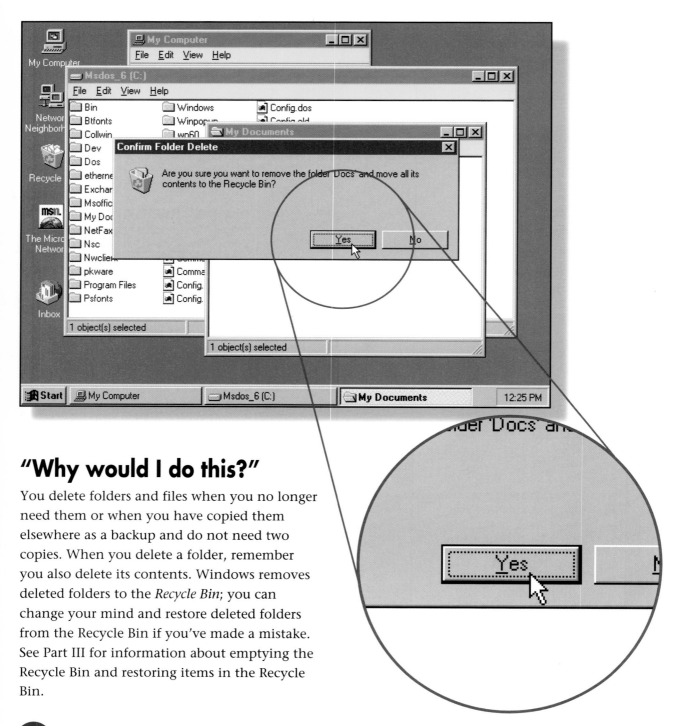

"Why would I do this?"

You delete folders and files when you no longer
need them or when you have copied them
elsewhere as a backup and do not need two
copies. When you delete a folder, remember
you also delete its contents. Windows removes
deleted folders to the *Recycle Bin*; you can
change your mind and restore deleted folders
from the Recycle Bin if you've made a mistake.
See Part III for information about emptying the
Recycle Bin and restoring items in the Recycle
Bin.

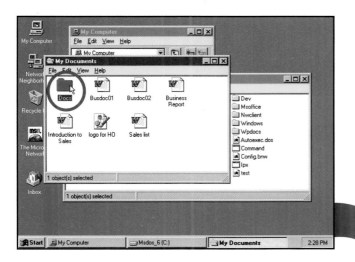

1 Select the folder you want to delete; it changes color.

NOTE ▼

To select multiple folders, hold the Ctrl key and click each folder you want to select. To deselect one folder of several, hold the Ctrl key while clicking on the folder you want to deselect. To deselect all folders, click anywhere in the window.

2 Open the **File** menu and choose the **Delete** command. A confirmation message appears.

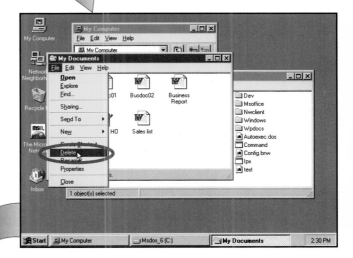

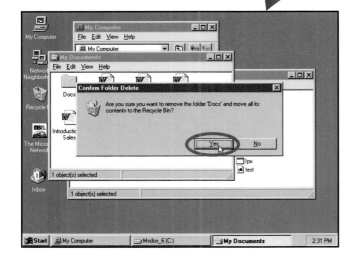

3 Choose **Yes** to delete the selected folder; the confirmation box closes and the folder disappears. ■

WHY WORRY?

If you change your mind about deleting the folder, choose the No button in the Confirm Folder Delete message box. The box closes and returns to the intact folder.

119

Finding Files and Folders

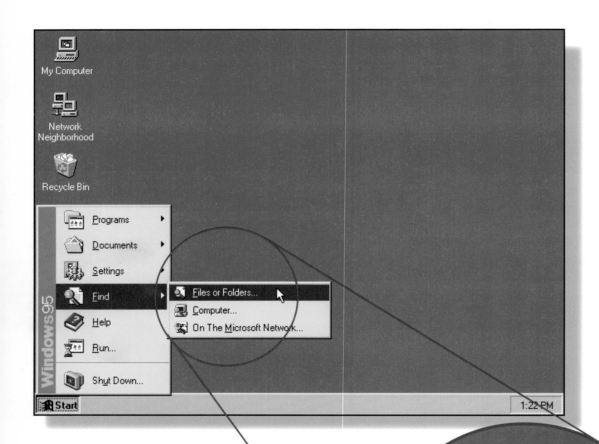

"Why would I do this?"

After working for months with your
applications, your computer becomes filled
with various folders and files, making it nearly
impossible for you to know where everything is.
Windows includes a command that helps you
locate specific files or folders by name, file type,
location of the file, and so on.

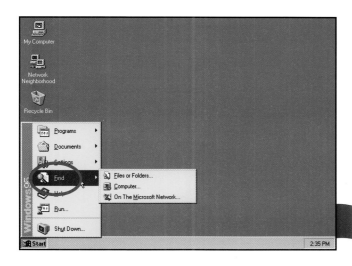

1 Open the **Start** menu and choose the **Find** command. A secondary menu appears. From the secondary menu, choose **Files or Folders**. The Find: All Files dialog box appears.

2 Choose the **Name & Location** tab. In the Named text box, enter the name of the file you want to search for.

> **NOTE** ▼
>
> You can use the characters * and ? (known as wild cards) in the search. For example, to find all files ending with the extension HLP, you could type *.hlp. You could type doc??.* to find all files beginning with doc followed by two characters and ending in any extension.

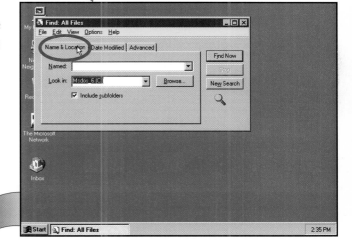

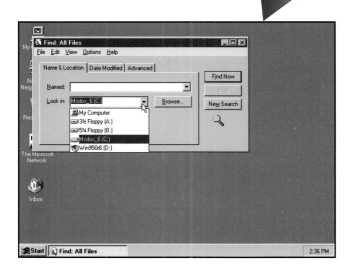

3 To change the drive of the search, click the down arrow next to the Look in list box and choose the floppy or CD-ROM drive from the drop-down list. If you want, you can choose **Browse** and then double-click on a specific folder in the Browse for Folder dialog box.

4 Click the **Find Now** button to initiate the search for the file name. Windows searches the hard drive, by default, and displays a list of found files at the bottom of the dialog box.

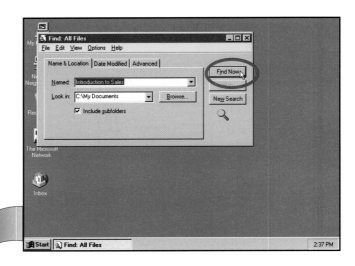

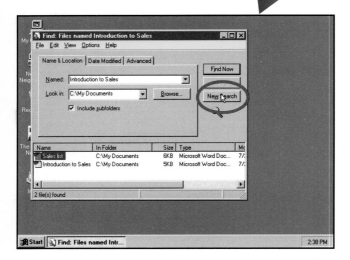

5 Click the **New Search** button to search for a new file or folder. A warning message appears stating the previous search will be cleared. Choose **OK**. The Find box appears, ready for the next search. To close the Find dialog box, click the **Close** button (**X**) in the title bar. ■

WHY WORRY?

If you do not know the name of the file for which you are searching but you know the type of file, choose the Advanced tab in the Find dialog box. From the Of type list box, choose the type of file, such as Application, Configuration, Help, MS Word Document, Text Document, and so on. Choose the Find Now button and Windows performs the search.

Managing Folders
with Quick Menus

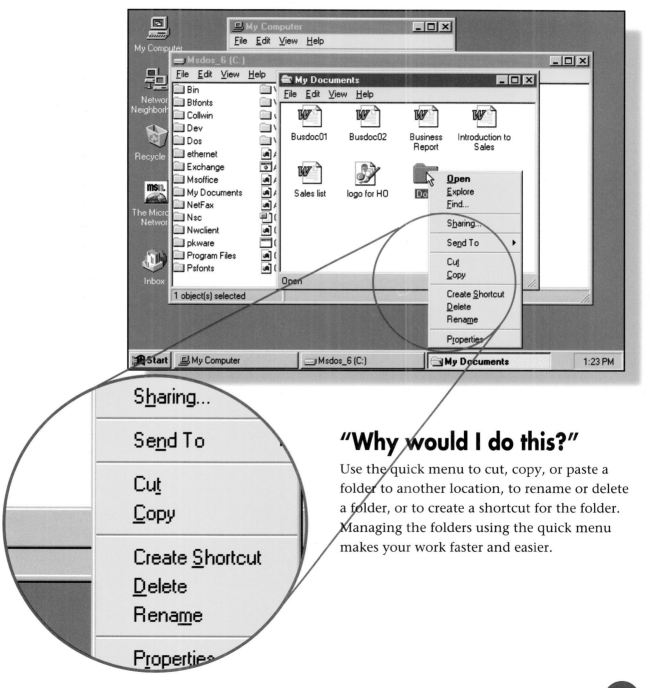

"Why would I do this?"

Use the quick menu to cut, copy, or paste a folder to another location, to rename or delete a folder, or to create a shortcut for the folder. Managing the folders using the quick menu makes your work faster and easier.

1 To display a folder's quick menu, point the mouse at the folder and click the right mouse button. The quick menu appears.

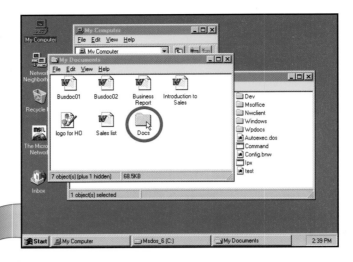

2 Choose **Send To** and a secondary menu appears. Choose to send a copy of the folder to a floppy drive and Windows copies the folder.

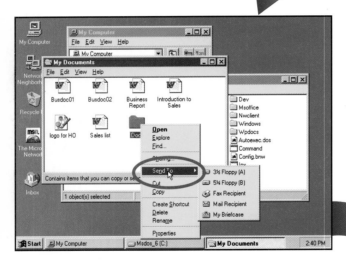

NOTE ▼

You can also choose to Cut or Copy a folder from the quick menu. Open another folder or drive on your computer and then choose the Paste command from the quick menu.

3 Right-click a folder to display the quick menu and then choose the **Rename** command. Windows selects the folder's name for you to rename; all you have to do is type in the new name.

Choose **Delete** on the quick menu to delete the folder and its contents.

Choose **Create Shortcut** on the quick menu to create a shortcut icon you can drag to the desktop for quick and easy access to the folder. ■

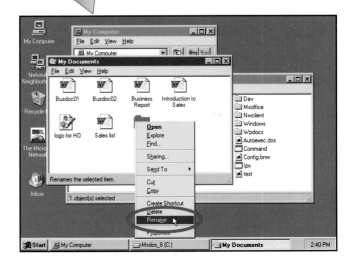

Using the Toolbar

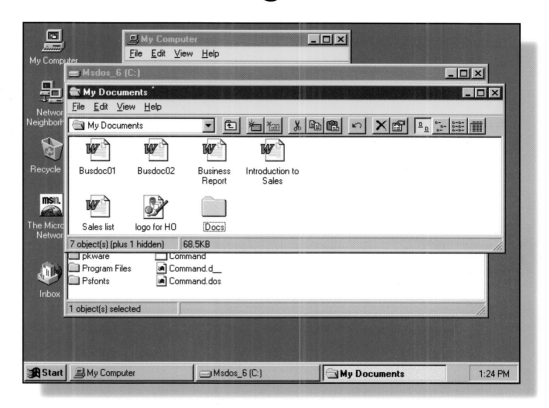

"Why would I do this?"

Each window, whether it's a file or folder window, includes a toolbar you can use to quickly change drives or directories in the window and to change views of the folder contents. (Note that the Windows Explorer displays this toolbar by default.)

1 Open the hard drive of your computer and then open the My Documents window. Folders represent any directories in the My Documents folder.

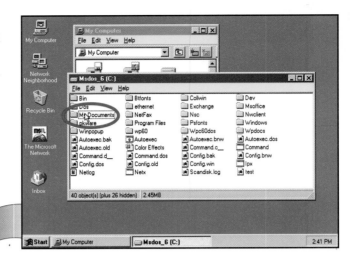

2 Choose the **View Toolbar** command, and a toolbar is added to the window. To view the entire toolbar, you may need to resize the window.

WHY WORRY?

You can edit the file while you're in the application and then choose File Save to save any changes you have made. To edit the file you are viewing in Quick View, choose File, Open File for Editing, and Windows opens the application used to create the file. You can then edit and save the file as you normally would.

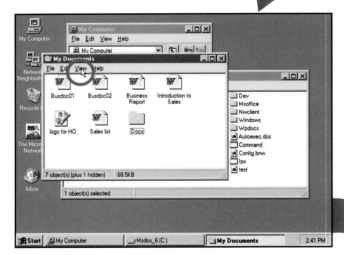

3 Click the down arrow next to the Go to a Different Folder list box to view available drives. You can change drives or you can work within the current drive. ■

WHY WORRY?

If you are not sure of what any button on the toolbar does, hold the mouse pointer over the button and a ToolTip appears, describing the function of the button.

Sorting Files

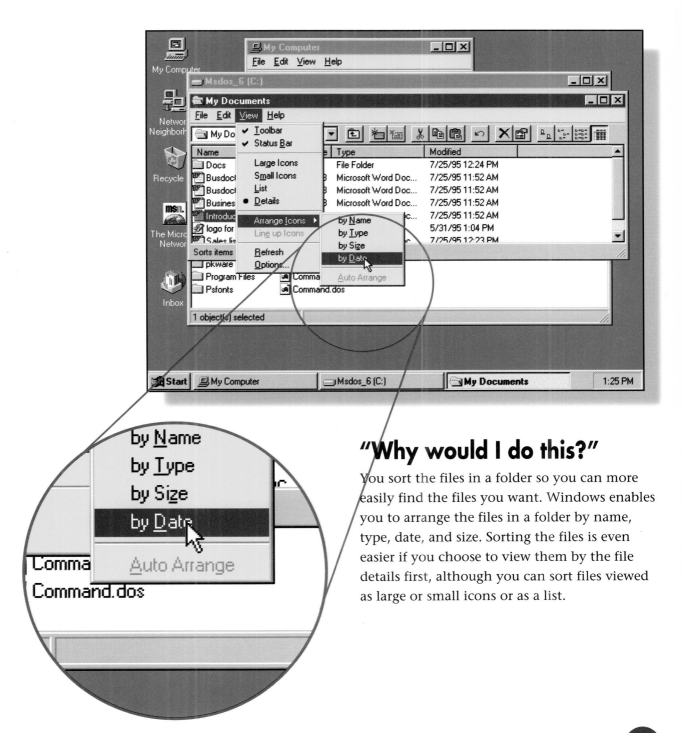

"Why would I do this?"

You sort the files in a folder so you can more easily find the files you want. Windows enables you to arrange the files in a folder by name, type, date, and size. Sorting the files is even easier if you choose to view them by the file details first, although you can sort files viewed as large or small icons or as a list.

1 Open the folder or drive containing the files you want to sort. Choose **View**, **Details** to list the file names, sizes, and types. Enlarge the window, if necessary, to see all of the file details.

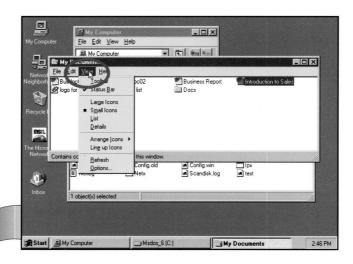

2 Choose **View**, **Arrange Icons** and a secondary menu appears.

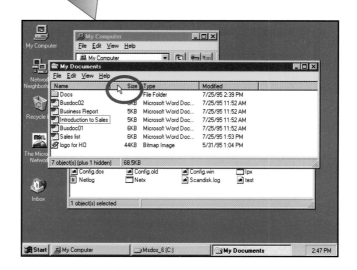

3 Choose **by Size** to sort the files from the smallest size to the largest. You can, alternatively, click the **Size** button above the list of files to sort by size; click the **Size** button again to sort the files from largest to smallest in size. ■

NOTE ▼

You can also sort by name in alphabetical order, by file type, or by date from oldest to most recent by clicking the specific command in the View menu, Arrange Icons command.

TASK 43

Copying and Moving Files

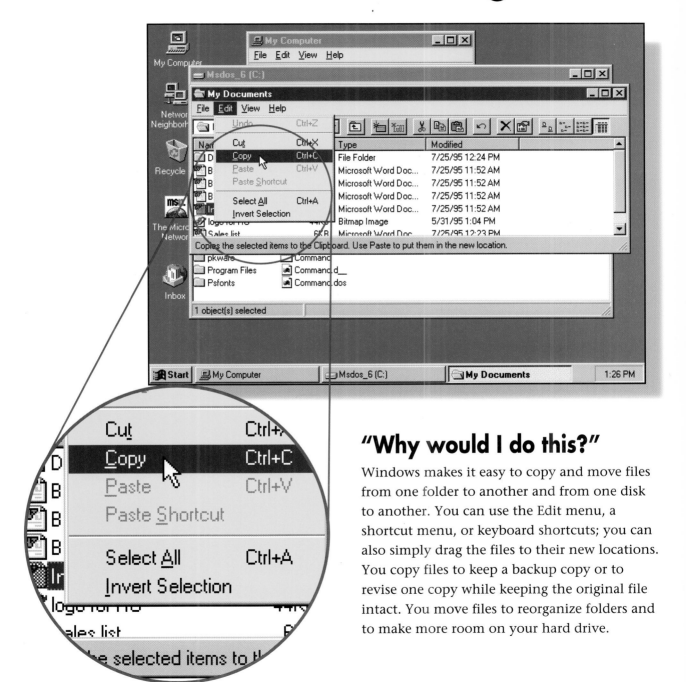

"Why would I do this?"

Windows makes it easy to copy and move files from one folder to another and from one disk to another. You can use the Edit menu, a shortcut menu, or keyboard shortcuts; you can also simply drag the files to their new locations. You copy files to keep a backup copy or to revise one copy while keeping the original file intact. You move files to reorganize folders and to make more room on your hard drive.

1 Select the file you want to copy. Choose **Edit**, **Copy** to duplicate the file or **Edit**, **Cut** to move the file.

> **NOTE** ▼
>
> To use drag-and-drop editing to move and copy files, open both the window that contains the file and the window for the folder or drive you want to copy or move the file to. To move the file, hold the Shift key while dragging a file to its destination. To copy a file, hold the Ctrl key while dragging the file to its destination.

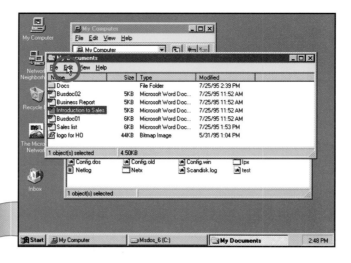

2 Select the folder, drive, or window into which you want to paste the copied or moved file and choose **Edit**, **Paste**. The file is moved or copied to the new location.

> **NOTE** ▼
>
> If you drag a file to a folder on the same disk, it will be moved; if you drag it to a folder on a different disk, the file will be copied.

3 To copy a file to a floppy disk, right-click the selected file. The quick menu appears. Choose **Send To** and choose the appropriate floppy drive. ■

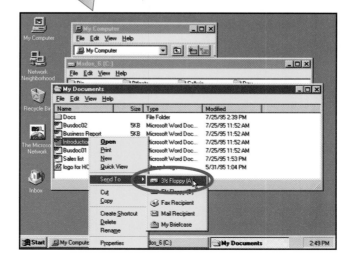

Deleting a File

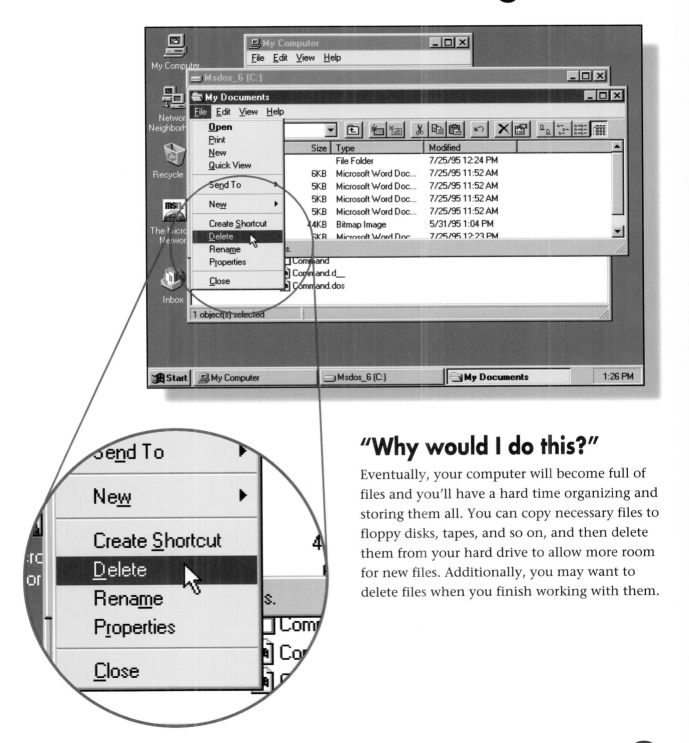

"Why would I do this?"

Eventually, your computer will become full of files and you'll have a hard time organizing and storing them all. You can copy necessary files to floppy disks, tapes, and so on, and then delete them from your hard drive to allow more room for new files. Additionally, you may want to delete files when you finish working with them.

1 Select the file you want to delete. Choose **File**, **Delete**.

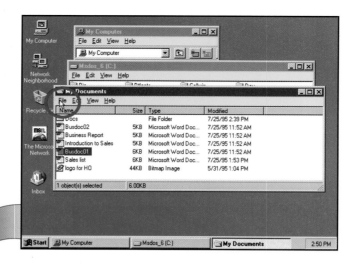

2 Windows displays the Confirm File Delete dialog box. Choose **Yes** to delete the file. Windows deletes the file to the Recycle Bin.

3 To empty the Recycle Bin, right-click the bin and the quick menu appears. Choose **Empty Recycle Bin**. Windows displays the Confirm File Delete dialog box again; choose **Yes** to delete the file. ■

WHY WORRY?

If you change your mind about deleting objects in the Recycle Bin, right-click the Bin and choose Open from the quick menu. A list of objects in the Bin appears. Select the item you want to keep and choose File, Restore. The file is placed back in its original location.

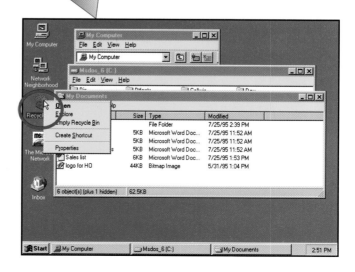

Using the Windows Explorer

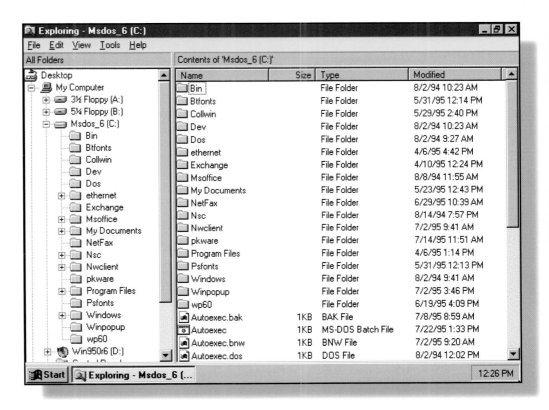

"Why Would I do This?"

You can use the Windows Explorer in much the same way you use the My Computer window: to copy and move folders, create and rename folders, view details, and so on. You might be more comfortable using the Explorer if you have used Windows 3.0 or 3.1; the Explorer in Windows 95 is very similar to the File Manager in previous versions of Windows. Alternatively, you may prefer the appearance of the Explorer to the My Computer window.

1 To open the Windows Explorer, open the **Start** menu and choose **Programs** from the menu. From the Programs menu, choose the **Windows Explorer**.

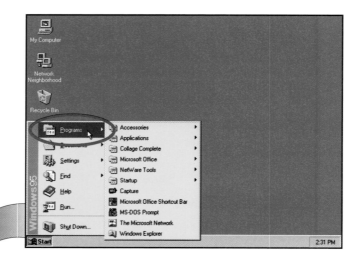

2 The left side of the split Explorer window lists all drives and folders on the hard drive. Any folder with a plus sign (+) in front of it represents a folder containing more folders and files. Click the folder and the folder's contents appear on the right side of the Explorer window. Double-click the folder and any folders it contains also appear under it on the left side of the window.

3 Double-click any folder on the right side of the Explorer window to display the contents of that folder. If you should double-click a file, such as a document file or program file, you would open that file and/or application. When you display folder contents on the right side of the Explorer window, file details are shown by default.

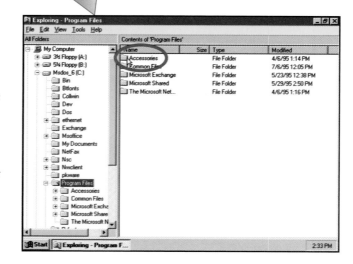

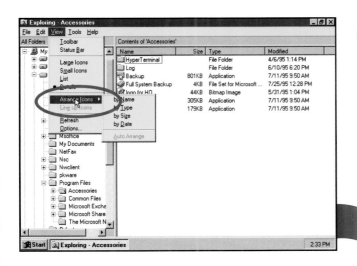

4 Choose **View**, **Arrange Icons** to sort the files by type, date, size, or name, just as you would in the My Computer window.

NOTE ▼

You also can choose View and show the files as large or small icons and display or hide the Toolbar and status bar of the Explorer window. Additionally, you can choose the Edit menu and cut, copy, and paste any folder or file, just as you would in the My Computer window.

5 Choose **Tools Find** and select **Files or Folders.** The Find: All Files dialog box appears. Search for any file or folder, just as described in Task 39.

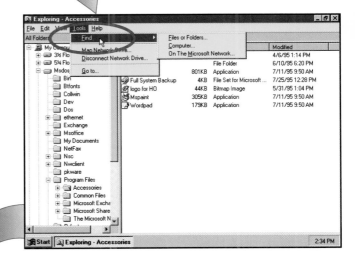

6 A handy feature of the Windows Explorer is copying files by dragging. Drag a file from the right side of the Explorer window to the left side, and drop it on top of the folder you want to copy it to. As you drag the file, a ghost of the file moves with the mouse; if you see a black circle with a line through it, that means you cannot drop the file at that particular location. When you release the mouse button, the file is dropped, or copied, to the last location of the mouse. ■

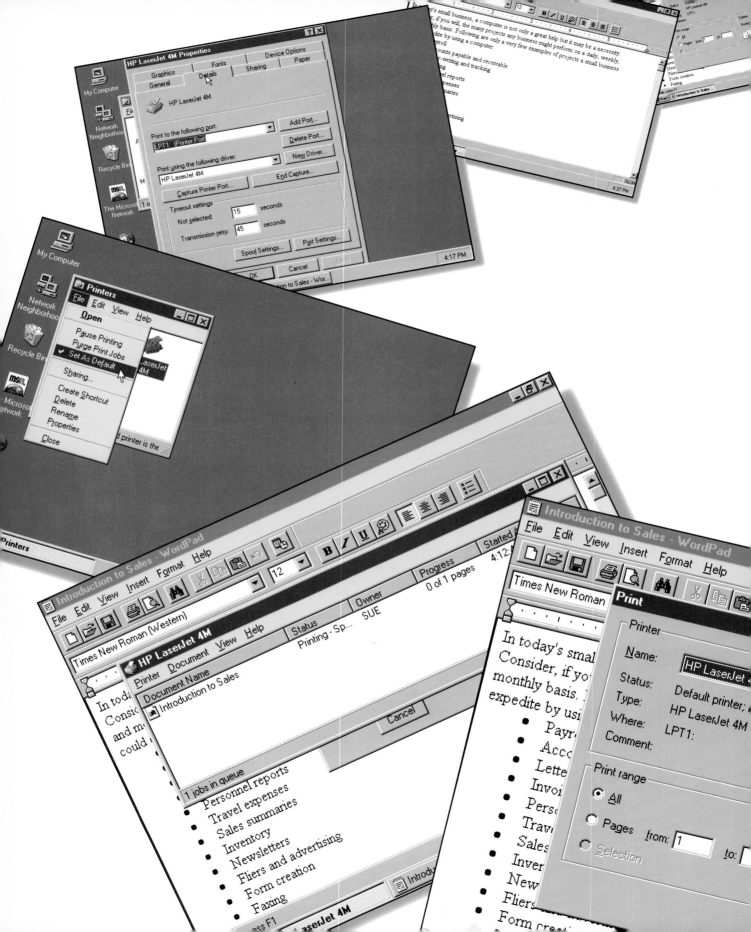

PART V

Printing with Windows

When you first install Windows, it configures your printer. All Windows applications use the same Windows configuration for your printer, saving time and ensuring you can print from any Windows application without reconfiguring for each program. Naturally, you can configure one or several printers in Windows and choose the printer you want to use at any given time. Additionally, you can easily manage printing for all of your applications through Windows.

You print a document from the application in which you created it; for example, if you produce a report in Excel or Word for Windows, you print the open document from that application.

When you send a file to the printer, the file first goes to a *print queue*, or holding area. Windows creates a print queue for each printer connected to your computer, and you can view files in the print queue before they are sent to the printer.

There can be one or many files in the print queue at any time, and Windows gives you control over them. While a file is in the print queue, you can pause printing, restart printing, and even cancel the printing.

In addition to managing the print queue and printing, Windows enables you to easily add printers to your computer by use of a step-by-step guide called a Wizard. The Wizard guides you through installing the hardware and any drivers that may come with your printer so you are sure the printer is configured correctly.

When you have two or more printers attached to your computer and con-figured in Windows, you can choose one to be the *default printer*. The default printer is the printer that you commonly use and that your applications will print to unless otherwise directed. It is a simple procedure to change which printer is the default printer. You can just as easily remove a printer as add one.

Finally, Windows enables you to easily change printer settings, such as the port and driver, as well as paper source, paper size, and orientation. Additionally, you can modify printer settings specific to your printer; for example, PostScript printers use options such as the level PostScript used and timeout values.

Windows makes configuring one printer for all Windows applications easy and efficient. This part shows you how to control and manage printing in Windows.

TASK 46

Printing a Document

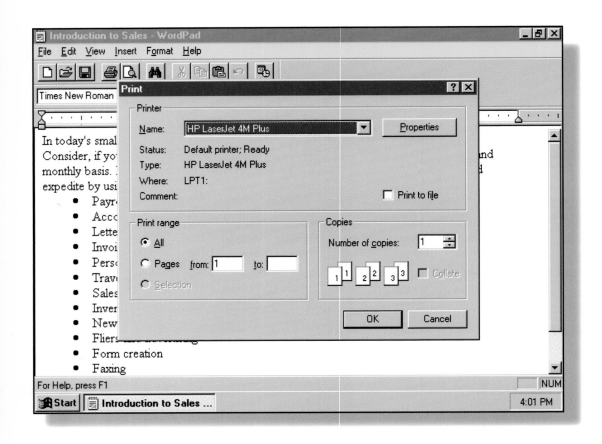

"Why would I do this?"

You can print documents from any Windows application, such as Word, Excel, Illustrator, and more, using the Windows setup for your printer. Printing your documents gives you a paper copy you can proofread, use in reports, give to co-workers, and so on. This task describes how to print.

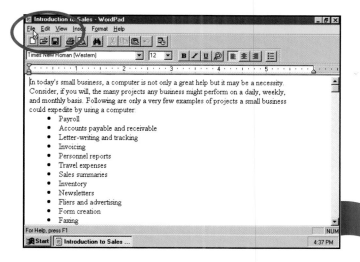

1 In the Windows application, open the **File** menu and choose the **Print** command. The application may also provide a shortcut such as the key combination **Ctrl+P**. The Print dialog box for the application opens. Each application's Print dialog box is slightly different yet they all work basically the same.

2 Enter the number of copies, the page range, and any other specific options. In Printer Name, choose the printer you want to use from the drop-down list, if you have more than one printer connected. Choose the **Properties** button to display a dialog box specific to the selected printer. From this dialog box, choose paper size, page orientation, specifics about printing graphics, and so on.

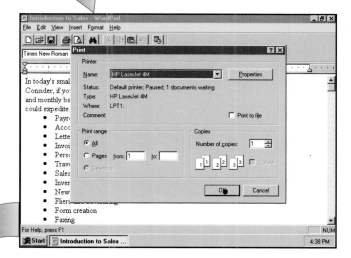

3 Choose **OK** to print the document. The Print dialog box closes and the document is sent to your printer. ■

NOTE ▼

You can create a shortcut for printing by opening the Printers folder from the My Computer folder. Right-click the printer icon and a pop-up menu appears; click Shortcut. Drag any document icon to the printer icon for quick printing.

Viewing the Print Queue

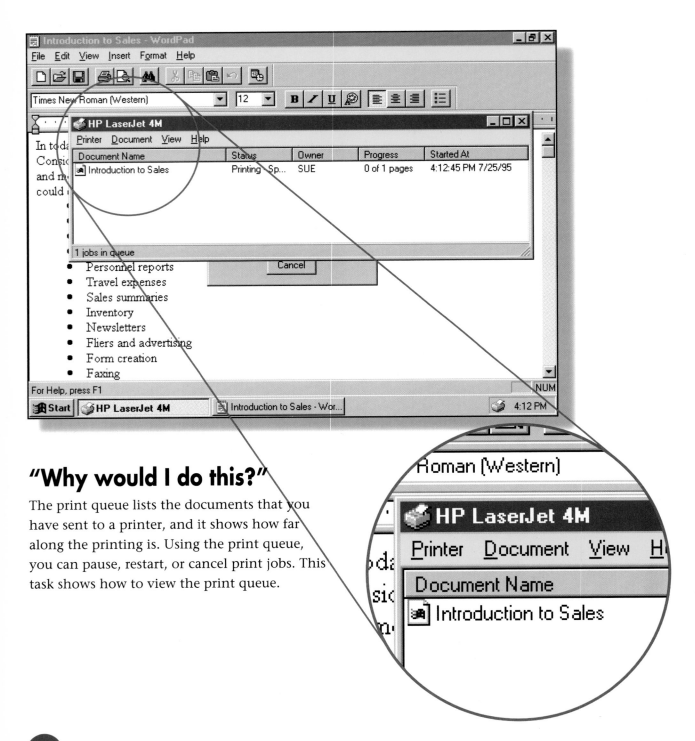

"Why would I do this?"

The print queue lists the documents that you have sent to a printer, and it shows how far along the printing is. Using the print queue, you can pause, restart, or cancel print jobs. This task shows how to view the print queue.

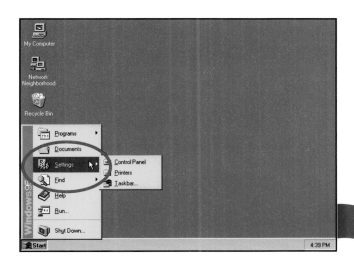

1 Open the **Start** menu and choose **Settings**. A secondary menu appears. From the secondary menu, choose **Printers**. The Printers window appears.

2 Double-click the printer whose print queue you want to view. The printer window opens with a list of the documents in the queue plus statistics about the documents being printed. If the window is empty, there is nothing in the print queue.

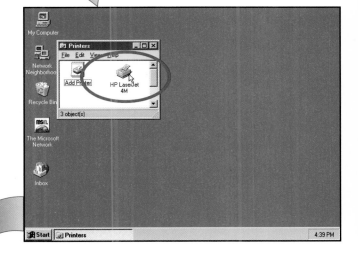

3 Using the Print Queue, you can pause printing one of many print jobs or all print jobs, as discussed in Task 49. You also can cancel printing in the Print Queue, as discussed in Task 50. To close the print queue, click the **Close** button (**X**) in the window's title bar. ■

Setting the Default Printer

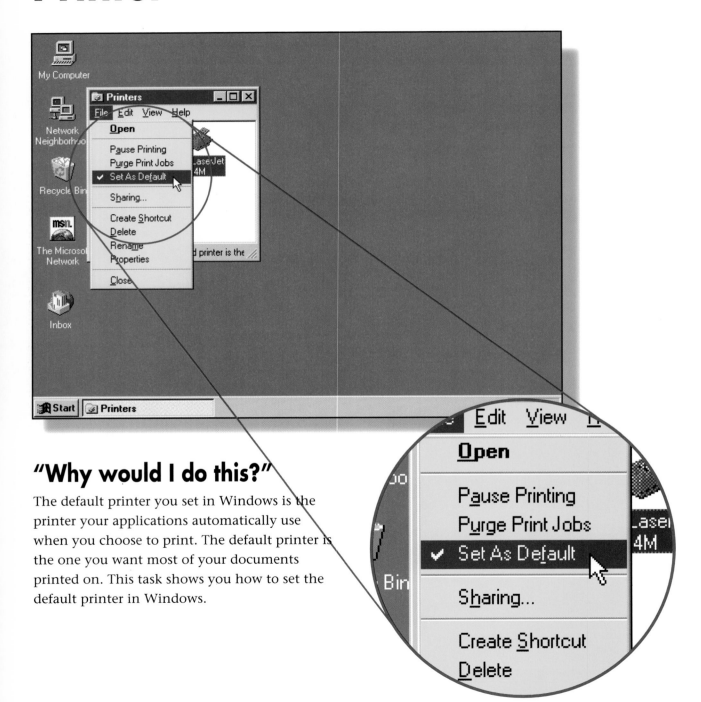

"Why would I do this?"

The default printer you set in Windows is the printer your applications automatically use when you choose to print. The default printer is the one you want most of your documents printed on. This task shows you how to set the default printer in Windows.

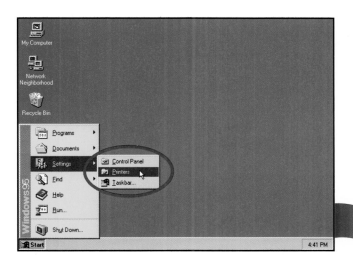

1 Open the **Start** menu and choose **Settings**. From the secondary menu, choose the **Printers** folder. The Printers window appears.

2 In the Printers window, select the printer you want to choose as default.

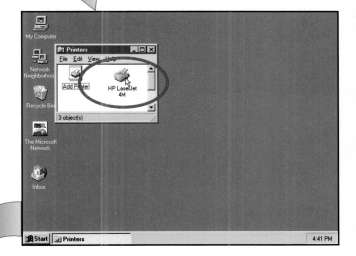

3 Choose **File, Set As Default**. You'll see a check mark beside this command whenever you select that particular printer and pull down the File menu. ■

145

Pausing and Restarting the Printer

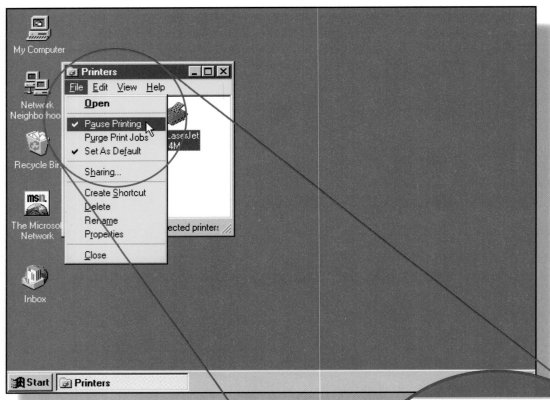

"Why would I do this?"

You may want to pause printing when you have a change to make in the text or when you want to load a different paper type, for example. You can stop the printing from the printers folder and then restart it at any time. This task describes pausing and restarting the printer.

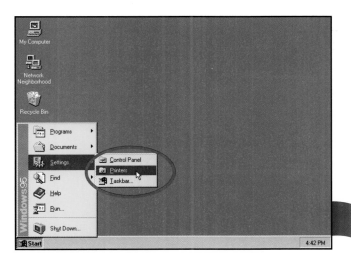

1 After sending the job to the printer, open the Printers folder by clicking the **Start** button and choosing **Settings**; then choose **Printers**. Select the printer to which you are printing.

NOTE ▼

Depending on your computer and your printer, the print job may only display in queue for a few seconds before it is sent to the printer.

2 Open the **File** menu and choose **Pause Printing**.

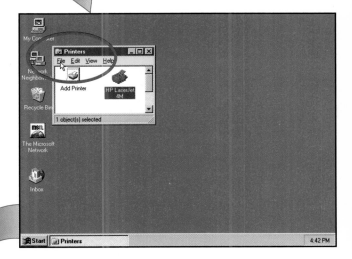

3 To restart the printing of a paused job, open the Printers folder and select the printer you want to restart. Choose **File**. The Pause Printing command has a check mark beside it; select the command to remove the check mark and continue printing. ■

Canceling Printing

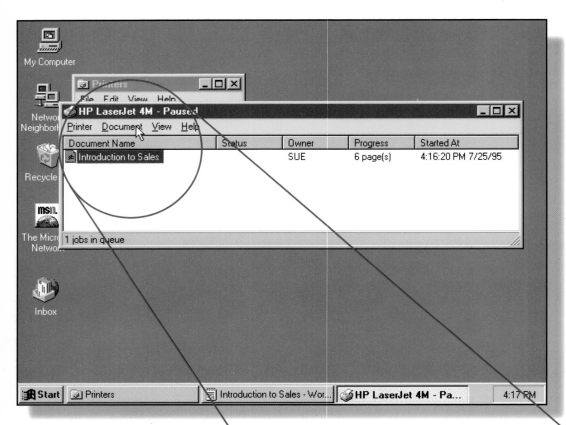

"Why would I do this?"

If you discover an error in the job you are printing or need to add something before printing the job, you can cancel the print job. Canceling the print job prevents you from wasting time and paper.

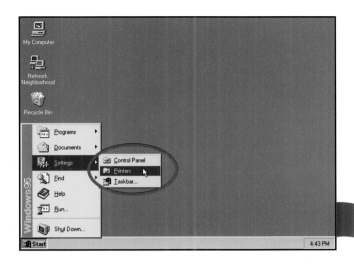

1 Open the **Start** menu and choose **Settings**. Choose the Printers folder. The **Printers** Folder window appears.

2 In the Printers folder window, double-click the printer to which the job has been sent. The print queue window for that printer opens.

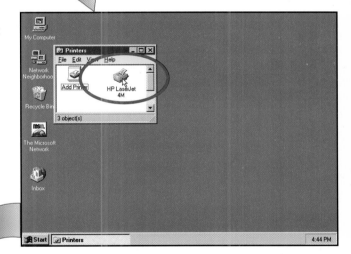

3 In the print queue, select the print job you want to cancel. Open the **Document** menu and choose **Cancel Printing**. ■

NOTE ▼

You can also use the Document menu in the print queue to pause printing on a specific job if several jobs have been sent to the printer. Select the job and choose Document Pause Printing.

149

Changing Printer Settings

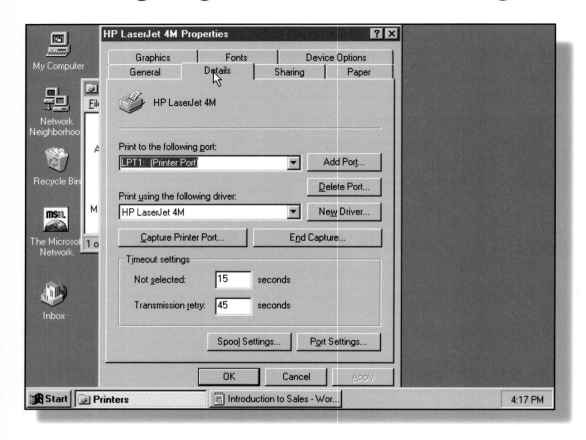

"Why would I do this?"

You can change printer settings, such as port, driver, and job priority as well as other settings specific to your printer. You might, for example, switch to a new printer driver so your printer works better with your applications; or you may change the port to which your printer connects to make room for other external devices, such as a modem or tape drive. Printer settings enable you to modify the way your Windows printer is set up and thus the way the printer responds to all Windows applications.

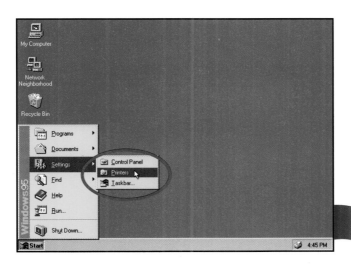

1 Open the **Start** me
and the **Printers**
folder window opens.

2 In the Printers folder window, select the
printer you want to change settings for;
open the **File** menu and choose
Properties. The Printer's Properties
dialog box appears with various tabs that
enable you to change settings.

NOTE ▼

Changing the printer's properties
changes them for all documents you
print on this printer. If you want to
change properties for just one
document, use the Page Settings
or Print Setup command in the
particular program.

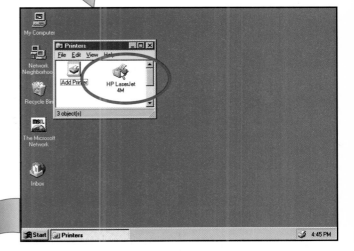

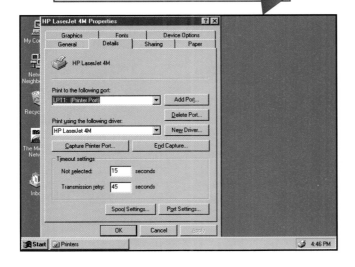

3 Choose the **Details** tab to change the
printer port, driver, timeout settings, and
so on. Note: the number and title of tab
settings on this screen will vary. Use the
drop-down list to select from common
ports. If you choose to print to a file,
Windows will prompt for a location and
file name. Choose which driver to use
from the drop-down list. You can also
choose to install a new
driver. Timeout settings
specify how long Windows
will wait before reporting
an error to you.

151

Choose the **Paper** tab to change the paper size, orientation, source, number of copies, and so on.

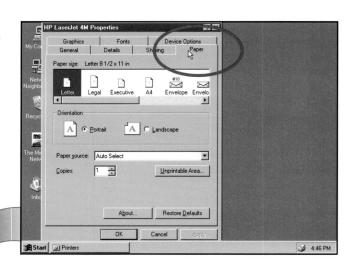

WHY WORRY?

If you make a change in the Paper, Graphics, Fonts, or Device Options tab and change your mind about the changes, you can choose the Restore Defaults button in that tab to cancel just that tab's changes.

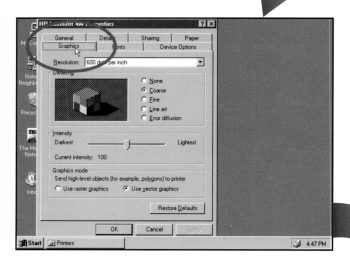

5 Choose the **Graphics** tab to change print resolution, dithering, shading intensity, and graphics mode.

NOTE ▼

Dithering blends colors into patterns or black and white into gray for smoother printing. You can choose from various options to show sharp edges (Line Art) or smooth edges (Fine). Choose vector graphics to speed up printing but create less detailed images; choose raster graphics to sharpen overlaid colors and details. Specify the intensity to tell Windows how dark or light to print the graphics.

6 To print a test page from the selected printer after making changes in the settings, choose the **General** tab and click the **Print Test Page** button. Click **OK** when you're finished. ■

NOTE ▼

The Fonts tab lists various cartridges you may have added to your printer. Choose the cartridge here to enable the use of the fonts in Windows. Also, install any printer fonts or new font cartridges. Use the Device Options tab to choose printed text quality; the available options depend on your printer.

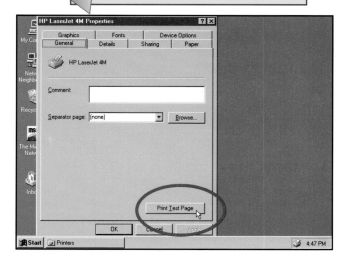

Adding a Printer

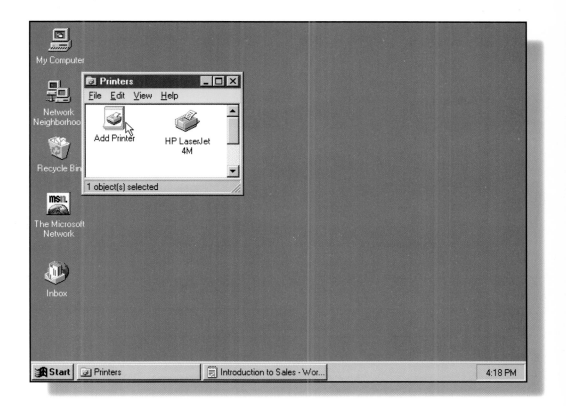

"Why would I do this?"

You can add a new printer to your Windows configuration using a step-by-step guide that Windows provides, called a Wizard. Use the Wizard when you get a new printer, change printers, or attach to someone else's printer.

1 Open the **Start** menu and choose the **Printers** folder and **Settings**; then choose **Printers**. In the Printers Folder window, double-click the **Add Printer** icon. The first box of the Add Printer Wizard appears.

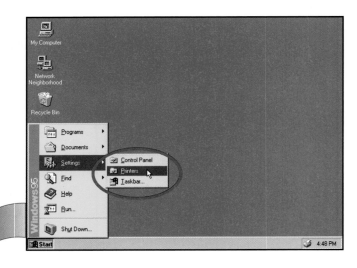

2 Choose the **Next** button to continue with the installation of the new printer. The second Add Printer Wizard box appears.

3 Choose the appropriate option for the connection of the printer, **Local** for example, and click the **Next** button. A different Add Printer Wizard box appears.

> **NOTE ▼**
>
> Depending on whether you choose Local or Network, the following Wizard boxes ask different questions. If you chose Network as the connection, follow the directions on-screen for the rest of the Wizard boxes.

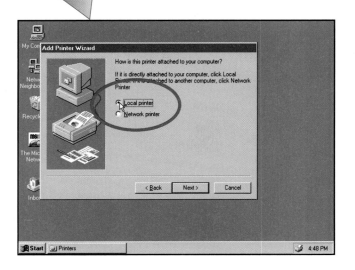

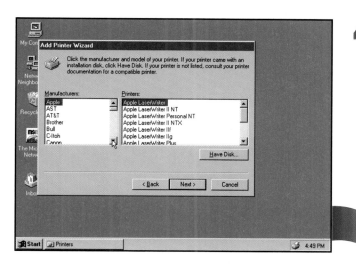

4 Choose the Manufacturers name and then select the Printers name. You can choose the **Have Disk** button and use the manufacturers disk to load the drivers or you can choose **Next** and Windows will prompt for the CD or disk to load its own drivers (see step 8). After you load the drivers or choose Next, the Add Printer Wizard box for setting the printer port appears.

5 Choose the appropriate port and select **Next**.

WHY WORRY?

You can cancel the process at any time by choosing the Cancel button in any of the Wizard dialog boxes. You can also choose the Back button in the Wizard boxes to move to the previous dialog box and review or modify your selections.

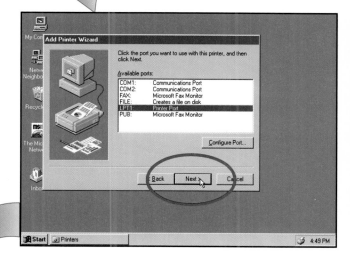

6 Enter a name for the printer or accept the one Windows has given it; also decide if you want the new printer to be the default printer. Choose **Next** when you finish.

7 Choose to print a text page in the final Add Printer Wizard box and click the **Finish** button.

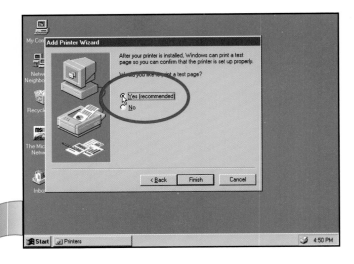

8 If you chose to use a Windows driver for the new printer in step 4, Windows prompts you for the disk or CD. Insert the disk or CD and enter the path in the Copy files from text box. Choose **OK** tocontinue adding the printer.

9 Windows displays a message box telling you it printed the test page and asking if it printed successfully. Choose **Yes** if it did. Windows then adds the new printer's icon to the Printer folder. ∎

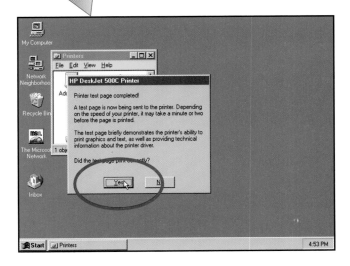

PART VI
Controlling Windows Fonts

A *font* is a complete collection of letters, punctuation marks, numbers, and special characters in the same typeface, such as Courier, Arial, or Times New Roman. Within each font is a variety of styles and sizes. Styles, for example, can be bold, italic, or bold italic. Sizes are measured in points and can be as small as 6- or 8-point or as large as 72-point or more.

A 72-point character is 1 inch tall, therefore, each point is the equivalent of 1/72 inch.

Bold

Italic

Underline

Windows uses fonts to display the names of folders, menu items, commands, titles in a window, dialog box items, and so on. The font typeface, size, and style used on the display are called *system fonts* and are usually a plain, easy-to-read font. You can, however, change the system font to personalize your display or to make the words on-screen easier to see.

Windows also provides fonts for special characters, such as the trademark and copyright symbols, pointing arrows, Greek letters, and so on. You can insert any of these special characters into your documents for a more professional-looking presentation.

Courier

Times

Shelley

In addition to displaying fonts and special characters, Windows provides fonts you use in your documents. You can choose from a variety of typefaces and styles and enlarge or reduce Windows fonts to suit your needs. Most applications list the available fonts from which you choose. Additionally, Windows includes a Font Folder in which you can list fonts, view sample fonts, and even add fonts to your list.

The fonts you have in Windows depends on several things. Windows provides basic font families: including Arial, Courier, Symbol, and Times New Roman. Within each of these families are a variety of styles and sizes. Any applications you add to Windows may provide additional fonts. Finally, your printer adds to the list of available fonts by providing two or more font families, depending on the type of printer you have.

The fonts Windows provides are called *TrueType fonts*. TrueType fonts offer a variety of typefaces, styles, and sizes for your documents. Additionally, with TrueType fonts, you get the ever popular "WYSIWYG" or what-you-see-is-what-you-get. WYSIWYG means the font you see on the screen is the actual font that prints from your printer. One of the advantages of TrueType fonts is that Windows can replicate the exact font you see on-screen to just about any printer; thus you should use a TrueType font whenever you have the choice. TrueType fonts are preceded by a **TT** on most font lists in applications.

Also included in any listing of fonts are *printer fonts*, usually represented by a small printer icon, and any other fonts in your system, such as Adobe fonts or Bitmap fonts. Depending on your printer, you may see an additional two or more fonts added to Windows. Printer fonts are those stored in your printer and available to you in your documents. The font you see on screen, however, may or may not be exactly what you get when the font is printed.

You can purchase add-on font disks containing TrueType fonts to install to Windows and use in your applications. After you install a font, it is available to all Windows applications.

This part illustrates how to use and manage Windows fonts.

Changing Display Fonts

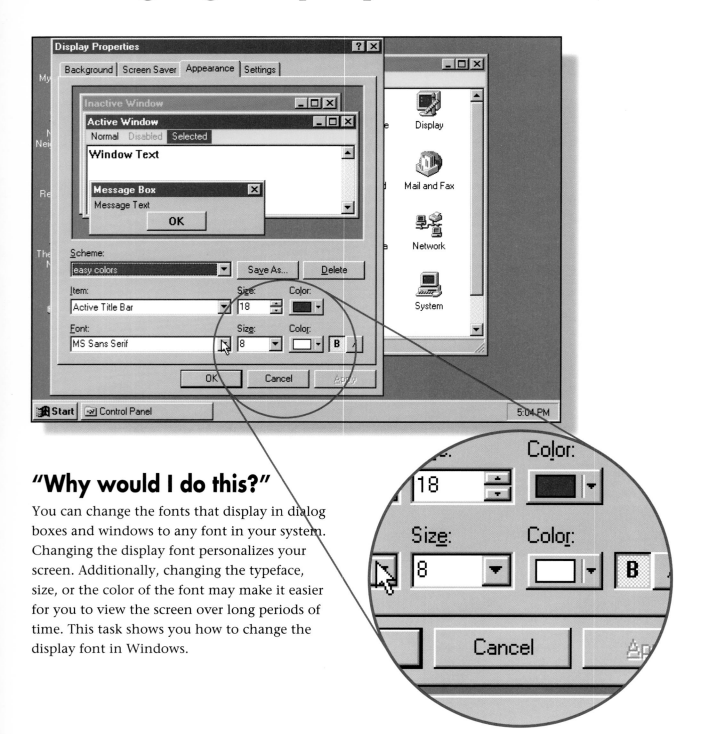

"Why would I do this?"

You can change the fonts that display in dialog boxes and windows to any font in your system. Changing the display font personalizes your screen. Additionally, changing the typeface, size, or the color of the font may make it easier for you to view the screen over long periods of time. This task shows you how to change the display font in Windows.

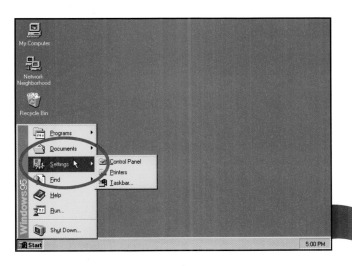

1 Open the **Start** menu and choose **Settings**. From the secondary menu, choose **Control Panel**. The Control Panel window opens. The Control Panel enables you to change settings, or customize, the way Windows works. You can, alternatively, open the Control Panel by double-clicking its icon in the My Computer window.

2 In the Control Panel, double-click the **Display** icon to open the Display window. The Display Properties dialog box appears with four tabs that offer options for changing your display: Background, Screen Saver, Appearance, and Settings. For more information on these tabs, see Part VII, "Personalizing Windows."

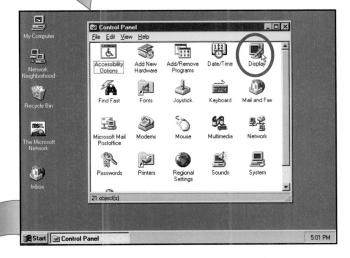

3 Choose the **Appearance** tab. The Appearance tab enables you to change fonts, color scheme, and so on, by clicking an area in the sample screen and then changing the item.

le screen, click the title bar
...the words **Active Window**. The
Item changes to **Active Title Bar** and
the default scheme, font, color, and so on
appear below the sample screen. Any
changes you make apply to the selected
item.

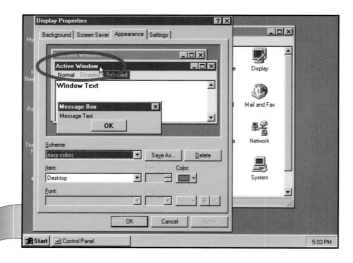

5 Click the down arrow in the **Fonts** drop-down list to display the list of available fonts. Select the font you want; for example, select **Times New Roman**. Notice the changes in the selected item.

WHY WORRY?

Don't worry; any changes you make in the dialog box can easily be revoked by choosing Cancel to close the Display Properties dialog box.

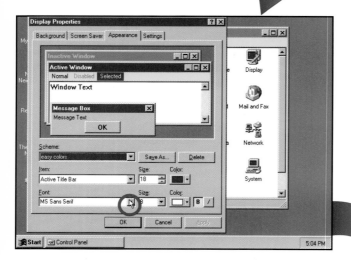

6 Click the **Size** down arrow to display a list of available sizes. Select the size you want. Note that you can also change the color of the font and the background by choosing an option from the Color drop-down lists. If you like the changes, choose the **Save As** button and name the color scheme. The font type and size also save with the color scheme. When you're happy with your changes, choose **OK**. ■

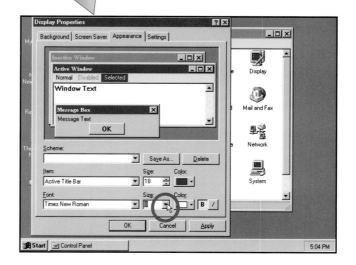

Inserting a
Special Character

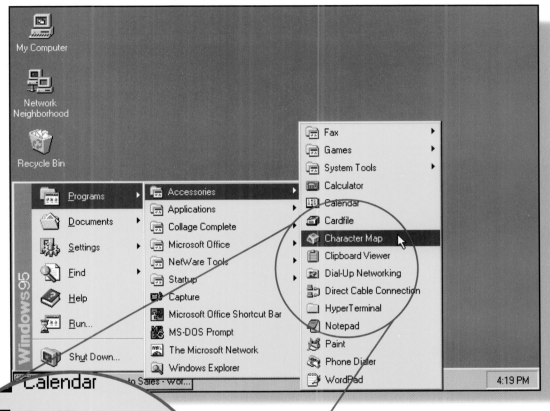

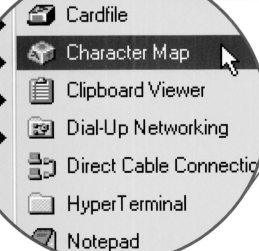

"Why would I do this?"

You can insert special characters, such as bullets, the trademark symbol, arrows, Greek letters, and so on into your documents. Special characters make your document look more professional and get your message across clearly.

1 Open the **Start** menu and choose **Programs**. The secondary Programs menu appears.

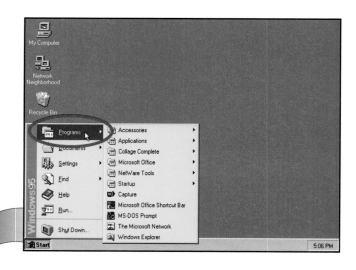

2 From the secondary menu, choose **Accessories**. The secondary Accessories menu appears. Choose **Character Map**. The Character Map window appears with a grid filled with various characters you can insert into a document.

3 Choose the font that has the characters you want to use from the **Font** drop-down list.

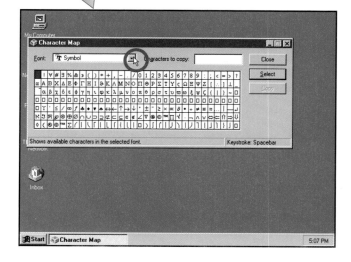

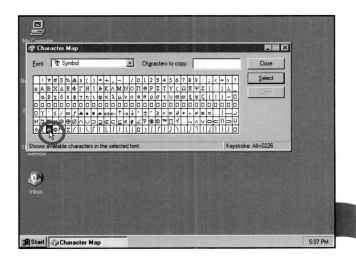

4 To view a character, point to the character, and press the mouse button and hold it down. The character enlarges so you can see it better. Release the mouse button when you finish viewing the character.

> **NOTE** ▼
>
> The Character Map displays a keystroke shortcut in the bottom right corner of the window. If it is a character you often use, remember the keystrokes and the next time you want to insert the character, press the keystroke instead of opening the Character Map.

5 Click the character you want and then click the **Select** button. The character appears in the Characters to Copy box. You can place as many characters as you want in the box before copying them.

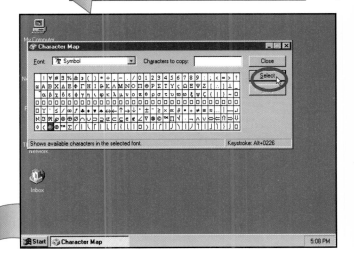

6 When you are ready to copy the characters, click the **Copy** button and duplicates of the character are placed on the Clipboard for you to paste. You can then open or switch to an application such as WordPad and paste the characters into a document by choosing **Edit**, **Paste**. To close Character Map, choose the **Close** button. ■

Viewing Fonts

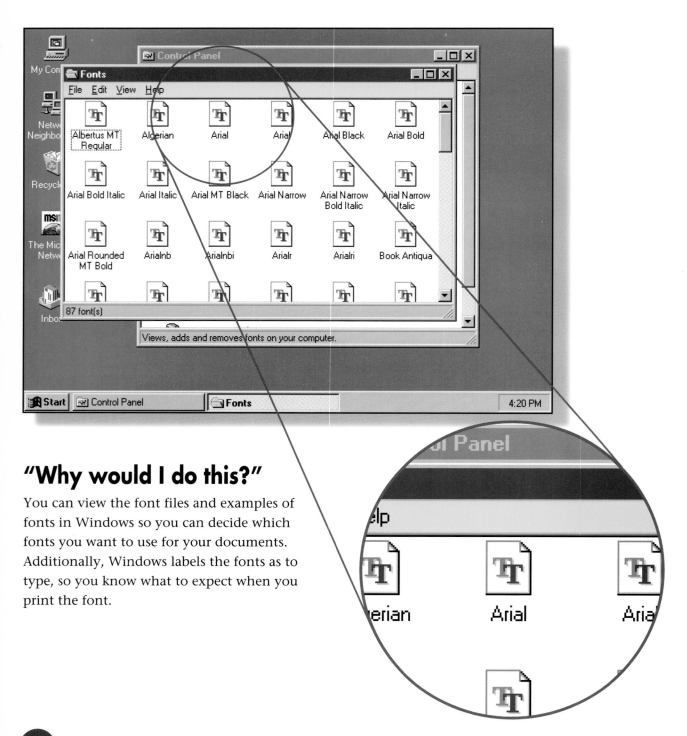

"Why would I do this?"

You can view the font files and examples of fonts in Windows so you can decide which fonts you want to use for your documents. Additionally, Windows labels the fonts as to type, so you know what to expect when you print the font.

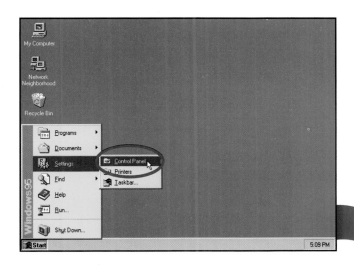

1 Open the Control Panel window by opening the **Start** menu, choosing the **Settings** command, and then choosing the **Control Panel**. The Control Panel window appears. In the Control Panel, double-click the **Fonts** folder; the Fonts window appears.

2 Note that the fonts represented by a **TT** are TrueType fonts. Double-click the icon for the font you want to view; for example, double-click the **Arial** font icon. The actual font and its available sizes display in a window.

NOTE ▼

You may also see an **A** icon, representing Adobe fonts, if you've installed Adobe Type Manager to your computer. Other icons may also display, depending on the types of fonts you have on your computer.

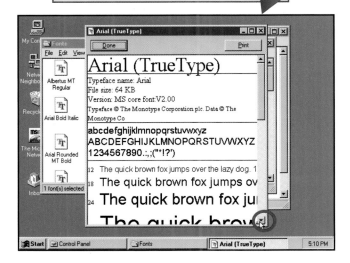

3 You can scroll to view more of the font, and you can even choose the **Print** button to print the sample. Click the **Done** button when you finish viewing the font. ▌

169

Adding Fonts

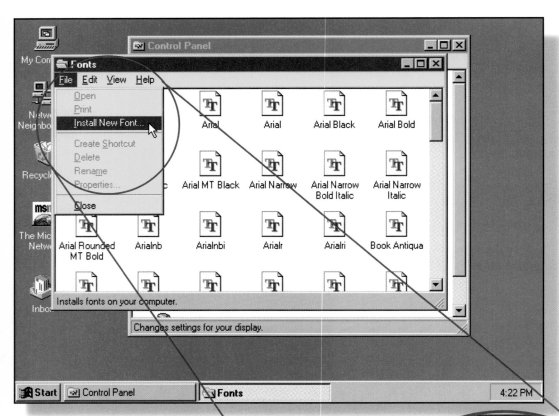

"Why would I do this?"

You can add a variety of fonts to Windows and then use them in any of your Windows applications. There are many fonts available that will help make your documents look attractive and professional.

1 Open the Fonts folder window from the Control Panel by choosing **Start**, **Settings**, **Control Panel**, and then double-clicking the **Fonts** folder.

2 Open the **File** menu and choose the **Install New Font** command. The Add Fonts dialog box appears.

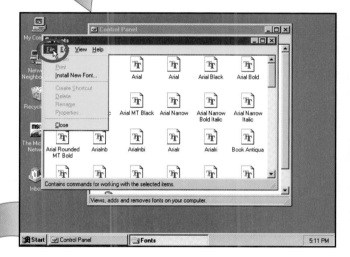

3 In **Drives**, choose the drive in which the fonts are located. Windows changes drives and lists available fonts in the List of Fonts box.

4 Select the font or fonts you want to install or choose the **Select All** button if you want to install all of the fonts on the disk.

> **NOTE** ▼
>
> Select successive files by holding the Shift key as you click the files you want. Select nonsuccessive files by holding the Ctrl key as you click the files you want.

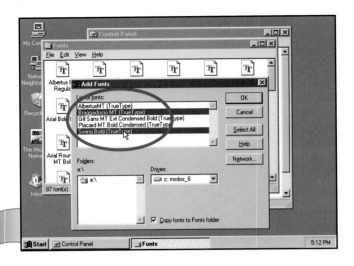

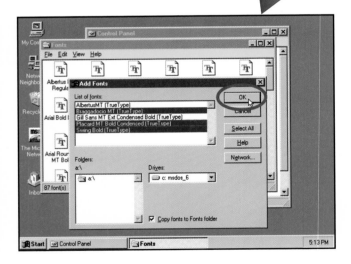

5 Choose **OK** in the Add Fonts dialog box. Windows copies the fonts to the Windows directory and adds the new fonts to the Fonts dialog box list, as shown in this figure. ■

> **NOTE** ▼
>
> TrueType fonts carry the TTF extension so they are easy to find on a disk. You also can install font files with a FON or FOT extension, among others.

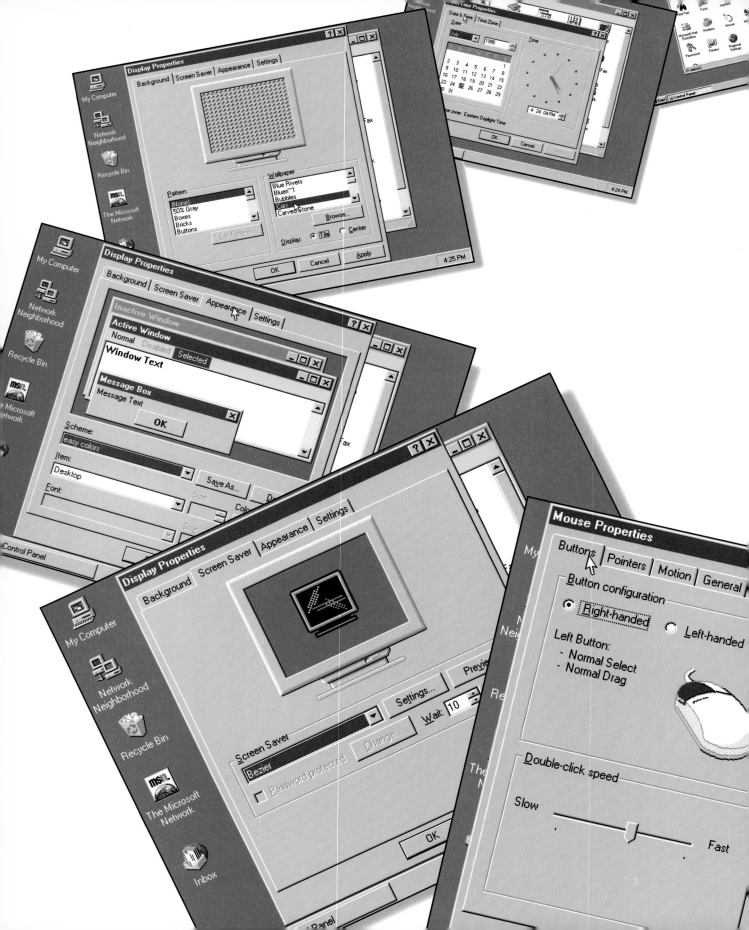

PART VII

Personalizing Windows

To make Windows a more comfortable and useful place for you to work, Microsoft has made it easy for you to customize the program. You can adjust colors, settings, and other options in Windows to suit your working style. The changes you make to the program affect how you work in your Windows applications as well; therefore, if you find you are not satisfied with any of the changes you make in Windows, it's easy to make changes again.

In Windows, you can customize such settings as the screen colors and appearance, mouse movement and use, items on the Start menu, and the system time and date. You can change any setting back to the default setting at any time; thus, no alteration is permanent.

You use the Control Panel to modify many Windows settings, including the display, mouse, date and time, keyboard, and so on. Each setting you can customize is represented by an icon in the Control Panel, and you can open each setting's icon to a dialog box.

One important item you can change in Windows is the date and time on your computer. If the date and time are wrong, saved files display the wrong date, which can cause problems when you are looking for specific files or doing backups. Additionally, many applications enable you to insert the system date into forms, spreadsheets, tables, and so on. If the date on your computer is wrong, inserting the date becomes useless. You can change the system's date and time in the Control Panel.

Another handy option you can change is the screen display. Windows enables you to change the background color on the display, wallpaper (patterns and images you use to decorate your desktop), and the color schemes used for application windows and dialog boxes. You can even set up one of Windows' screen savers to run automatically—a screen saver is patterns that move across your screen so the monitor does not burn out over a period of time.

Additionally, you can change how your mouse works with Windows. Change the buttons if you are left-handed, slow the double-click speed, change the appearance of the pointer, and so on. Since you often use the mouse with Windows and Windows applications, you want to be comfortable with the mouse and its workings.

Finally, Windows enables you to add or remove applications from the Start menu to make it more convenient for the way you work. You can, for instance, add a program you often use to the top of the Start menu, or you can add any applications you want to the Programs menu.

Windows makes it easy for you to customize the desktop and other settings so you are more comfortable with your working environment. This part shows you how to customize Windows.

Opening the Control Panel

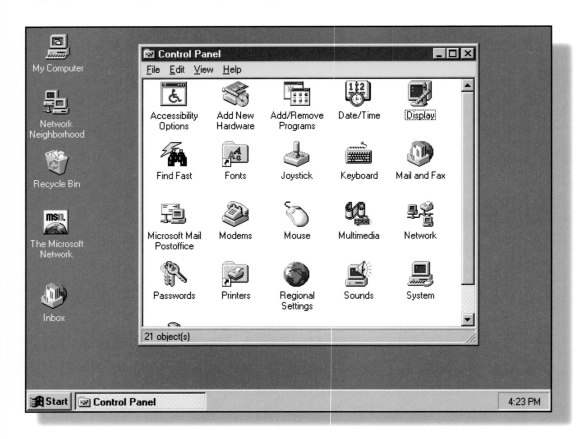

"Why would I do this?"

The Control Panel contains many settings you use to modify your Windows environment. You can open the Control Panel from the My Computer window or from the Start menu. This task shows you how to open the Control Panel window so that you can modify common settings.

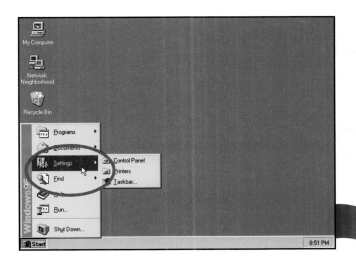

1 Open the **Start** menu and choose the **Settings** command. From the secondary menu, choose the **Control Panel**. The Control Panel window opens.

2 Alternatively, open the My Computer window by double-clicking the **My Computer** icon on the desktop. Then double-click the **Control Panel** folder. The Control Panel window opens.

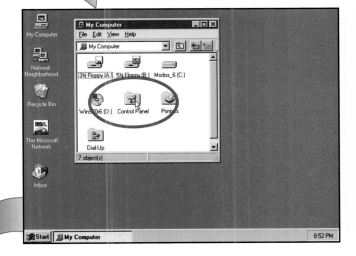

3 You can open any file in the Control Panel window by double-clicking the file's icon. To close the Control Panel, click the **Close** button (**X**) in the title bar. ■

Changing the System Date and Time

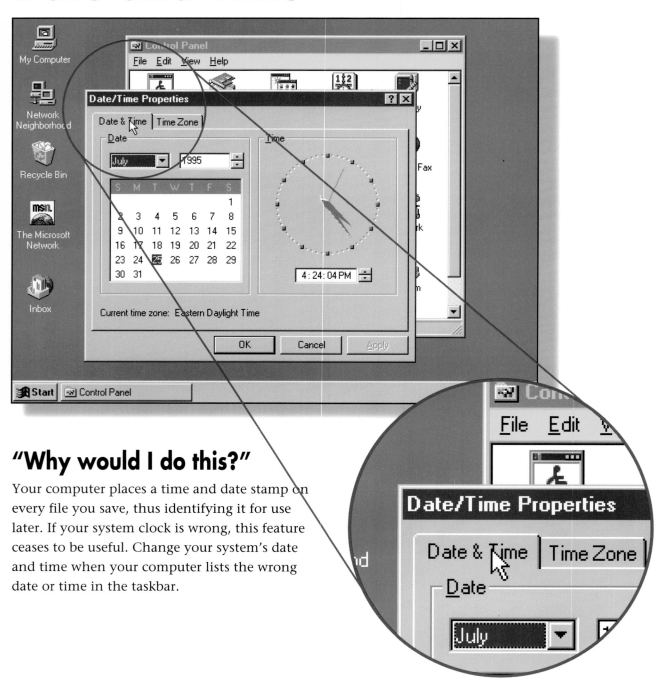

"Why would I do this?"

Your computer places a time and date stamp on every file you save, thus identifying it for use later. If your system clock is wrong, this feature ceases to be useful. Change your system's date and time when your computer lists the wrong date or time in the taskbar.

1 Open the Control Panel window and then double-click the **Date/Time** icon. The Date/Time Properties dialog box appears. If the Date & Time tab is not showing, select it.

NOTE ▼

You can also display the Date/Time Properties dialog box by double-clicking the time area on the taskbar.

2 In the Date & Time tab, click the correct date on the calendar and the date changes. If the month is wrong, click the down arrow to display the drop-down list and select the correct month. If the year is incorrect, type the correct one in the appropriate text box or use the up and down arrows to adjust the year.

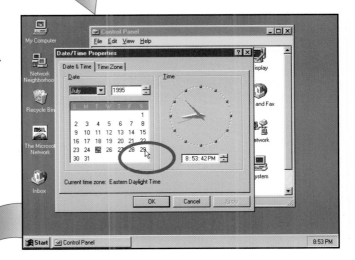

3 In the Time area, use the up or down arrows to adjust the time, or select and delete the current time and enter in the correct time. Make sure you use the same format: *hour:minutes:seconds* and *AM* or *PM*. Choose **Apply** and then choose **OK** to accept the changes and close the dialog box. ■

WHY WORRY?

If the date is wrong the next time you start your computer, you may have a dead battery. Replace it.

181

Customizing the Desktop's Background

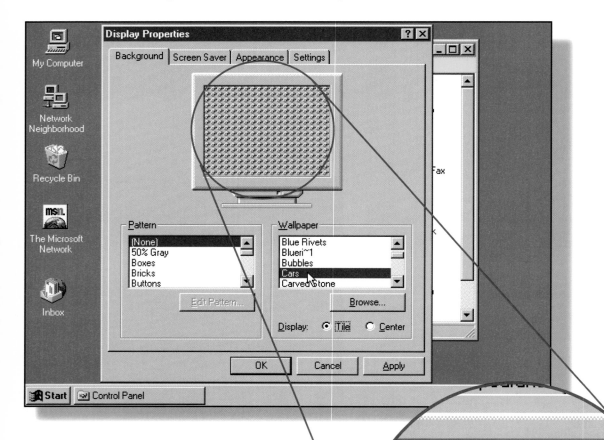

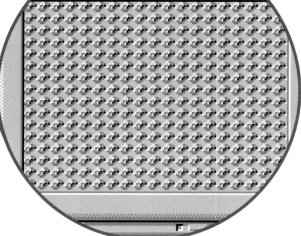

"Why would I do this?"

You can change the desktop in Windows by adding various patterns and wallpaper to make your working area more enjoyable. Windows offers paisley, tulip, waffle, and box background patterns, among others, as well as colorful car, honeycomb, square, and zigzag wallpaper patterns, and more. Choose any of these as a background for the desktop, or choose none for a calmer effect.

1 Open the **Control Panel** window and double-click the **Display** icon. The Display Properties dialog box appears with the Background tab showing; if the Background tab is not showing, choose it now.

2 To select a pattern, click one in the Pattern list; for example, click on **Boxes**. The pattern appears on the sample monitor. To have the pattern fill the desktop, choose Apply and then choose **OK**. Choose **(None)** to remove the pattern.

NOTE ▼

Wallpaper and patterns generally slow the speed of your computer and tax its memory. If your applications seem too slow after you display wallpaper or patterns, go back into the Display Properties dialog box and choose (None).

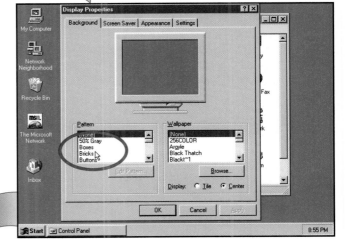

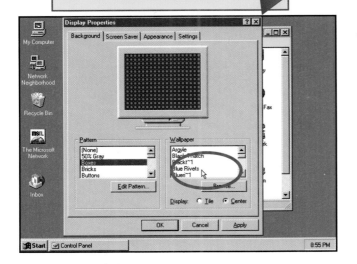

3 To choose wallpaper, select one from the Wallpaper list. The one you select appears on the sample monitor. If you see only one small image in the center of your screen, select the **Tile** option button to fill the screen with the wallpaper image. Choose **(None)** if you prefer no wallpaper. Choose **Apply** and then choose **OK** to accept the changes. ■

TASK 60

Changing Color Schemes

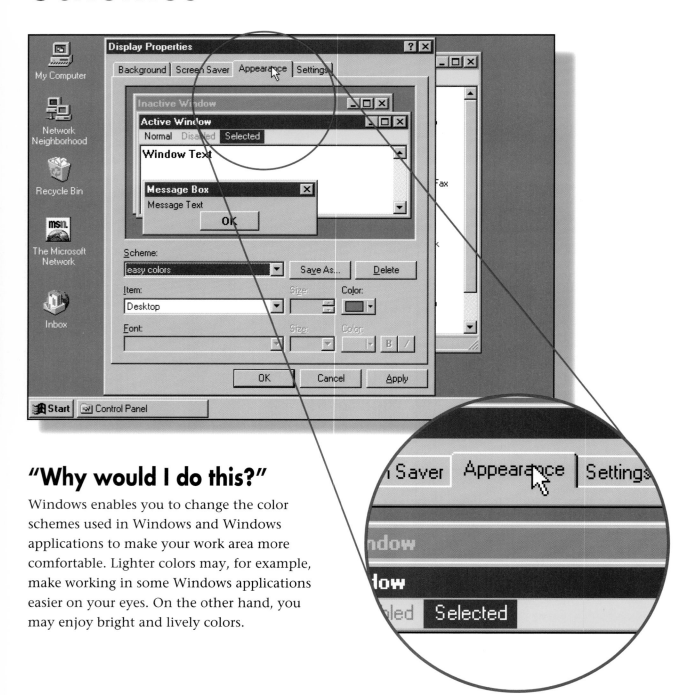

"Why would I do this?"

Windows enables you to change the color schemes used in Windows and Windows applications to make your work area more comfortable. Lighter colors may, for example, make working in some Windows applications easier on your eyes. On the other hand, you may enjoy bright and lively colors.

1 Open the **Control Panel** window and double-click the **Display** icon. The Display Properties dialog box appears. Choose the **Appearance** tab.

2 Display the Scheme drop-down list by clicking the down arrow. Choose any of the available color schemes. The color scheme appears in the sample box.

WHY WORRY?

If you cannot remember the original color scheme, simply choose the Cancel button to void all changes you made.

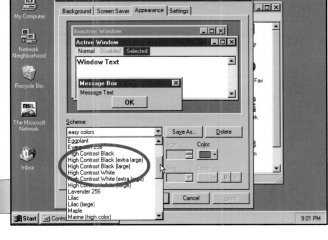

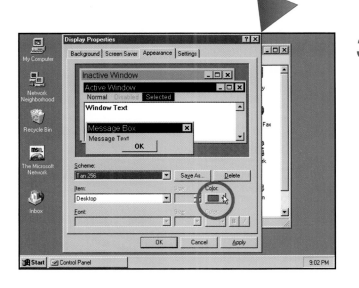

3 After changing the scheme, you can choose a different background color for the desktop in the Color list at the bottom of the dialog box. Additionally, you can change any item's color by first clicking the item and then selecting a different color from the Color list. Choose **Apply** and then choose **OK** to accept the changes. Choose **Save As** and name a new color scheme for later use. ■

Using a Screen Saver

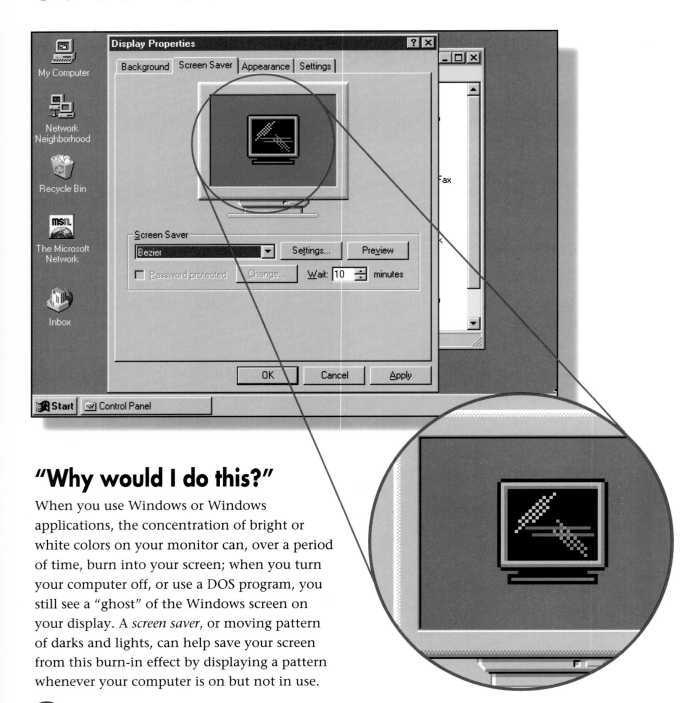

"Why would I do this?"

When you use Windows or Windows
applications, the concentration of bright or
white colors on your monitor can, over a period
of time, burn into your screen; when you turn
your computer off, or use a DOS program, you
still see a "ghost" of the Windows screen on
your display. A *screen saver*, or moving pattern
of darks and lights, can help save your screen
from this burn-in effect by displaying a pattern
whenever your computer is on but not in use.

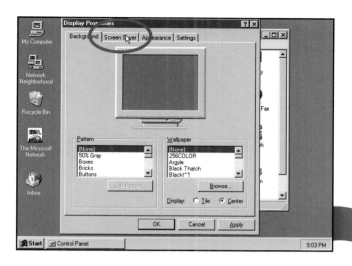

1 Open the **Control Panel** window and double-click the **Display** icon. The Display Properties dialog box appears; choose the **Screen Saver** tab.

2 Under Screen Saver, click the down arrow to display the list of available screen savers. Choose an option and view it on the example monitor.

NOTE ▼

If you want to see the screen saver on the full screen, choose the Preview button and Windows displays the entire screen with the saver. Click the mouse or press the Spacebar to return to the dialog box.

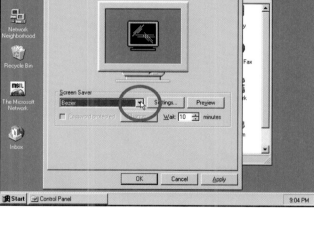

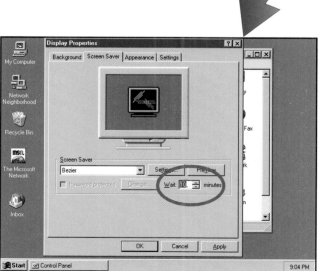

3 In the Wait text box, enter the number of minutes you want Windows to wait before it starts the screen saver. If, for example, you enter 10, when no one touches your keyboard or mouse for ten minutes, Windows starts the screen saver, which will continue until you move your mouse or hit a key.

4 With any screen saver selected, choose the **Settings** button to display the Setup dialog box. Each screen saver's setup dialog box is different. Experiment with the settings and choose **OK** to return to the Display Properties dialog box.

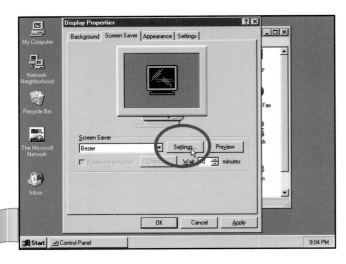

5 Click the **Preview** button to view the changes. Windows displays the entire screen with the saver. Click the mouse or press the **Spacebar** to return to the dialog box.

6 When you are satisfied with the changes to the screen saver, choose **OK** in the Display Properties dialog box. ∎

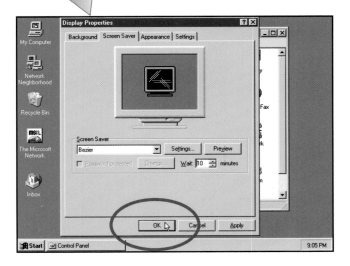

Adjusting the Mouse

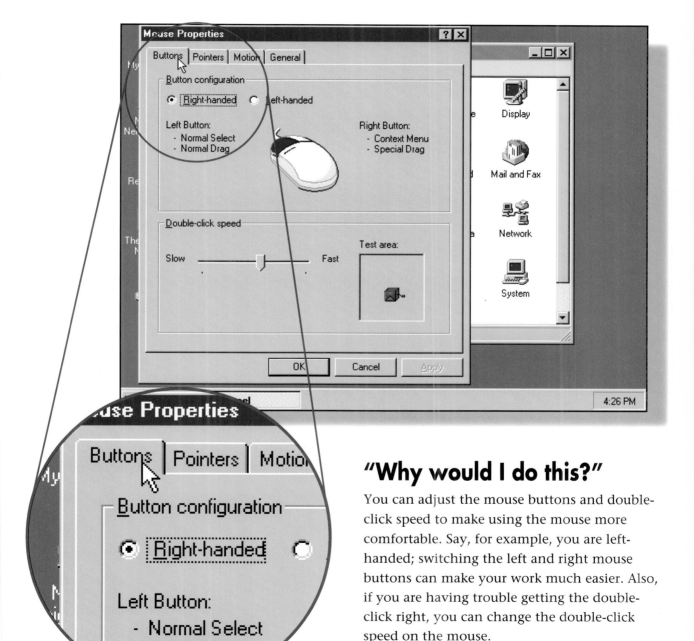

"Why would I do this?"

You can adjust the mouse buttons and double-click speed to make using the mouse more comfortable. Say, for example, you are left-handed; switching the left and right mouse buttons can make your work much easier. Also, if you are having trouble getting the double-click right, you can change the double-click speed on the mouse.

1 Open the **Control Panel** window and double-click the **Mouse** icon. The Mouse Properties dialog box appears. Choose the **Buttons** tab.

2 If you want to switch the mouse buttons, select the **Left-handed** option button in the Button configuration area.

3 To change the double-click speed, drag the lever between Slow and Fast. Test the double-click speed in the Test box. When you double-click correctly, a jack-in-the-box pops out. Double-click again and Jack goes back into the box.

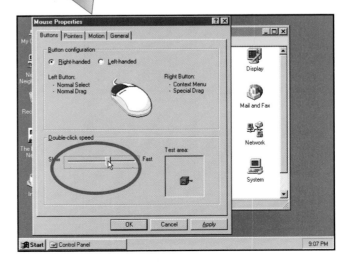

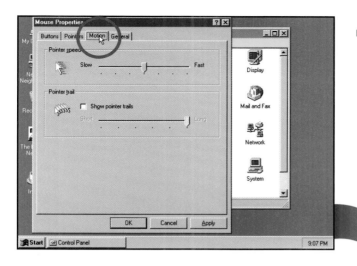

4 Choose the **Motion** tab to change the pointer speed or to leave a mouse trail. You may, for example, want to slow your pointer speed down so you can easily find your mouse on-screen when you move it quickly. Adjust the two options by dragging the lever between **Slow** and **Fast** for Pointer Speed and by dragging the lever between **Short** and **Long** after checking the Show Pointer Trails option.

5 In the General tab, change the mouse by clicking the **Change** button. You would change the mouse in this tab only if you buy a new or different mouse for your computer. Follow the directions on-screen after choosing **Change**.

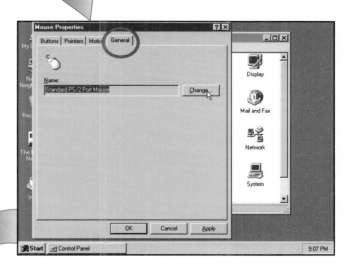

6 In the Pointers tab, you can change the appearance of a pointer. Select the pointer and choose **Browse**. In the Browse dialog box, choose a different filename to apply to the pointer. In **Scheme**, choose to use Animated Hourglasses if you want to use an hourglass pointer that moves as it displays.

When you finish with the mouse settings, choose **OK** to accept the changes and close the dialog box; choose **Cancel** if you do not want to save the changes. ■

TASK 63

Changing the Start Menu

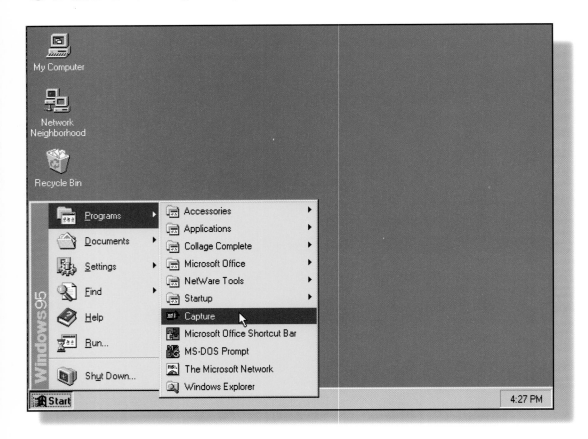

"Why would I do this?"

You can add programs to the Start menu to
make it more convenient to use. For example,
you may want to add programs that you use
often to the Start menu so that you can access
them more quickly.

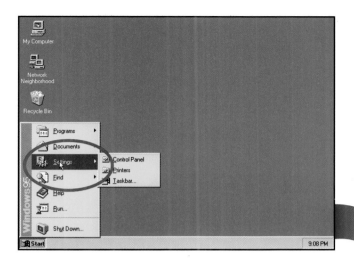

1 Open the **Start** menu and choose the **Settings** command. Choose the **Taskbar** command. The Taskbar Properties dialog box appears.

2 Choose the **Start Menu Programs** tab. To add a program to the Start menu, click **Add**. The Create Shortcut dialog box appears.

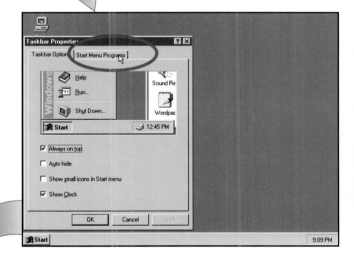

3 Choose **Add**. In the Create Shortcut dialog box, enter the Command line for the program you want to add in the text box. Choose the **Next** button and the Select Program Folder dialog box appears.

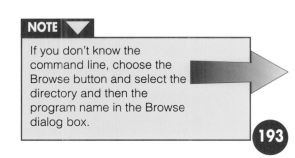

NOTE ▼

If you don't know the command line, choose the Browse button and select the directory and then the program name in the Browse dialog box.

193

4 Choose the folder in which you want to place the program. Choose **Next** and the Select a Title for the Program box appears.

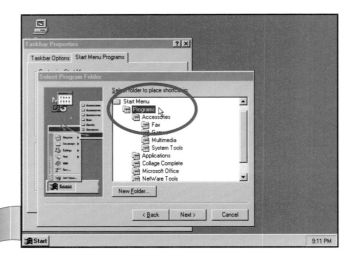

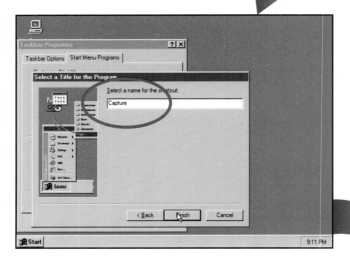

5 Enter a name in the text box or accept the one Windows displays. Choose the **Finish** button.

6 Open the **Start** menu and choose **Programs**. The added program now appears in the Programs menu. ■

WHY WORRY?

If you want to remove a program from the Start menu, go back into the Settings menu and choose Taskbar. In the Start Menu Programs tab, choose Remove and select the program from the list. Choose Remove, Close, and then choose OK to close the Taskbar Properties dialog box.

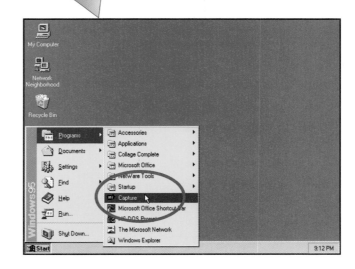

PART VIII

Sharing Data with Windows

ne of the biggest advantages of using Windows and Windows applications is that you can easily and efficiently share data—text, figures, pictures, lists, and so on—between the applications. Whether you are working with word processing or spreadsheets, databases or drawing programs, you can share the data in all of your Windows applications.

Windows makes it easy for you to open several applications at once and switch between them using the taskbar. Furthermore, you can open and view two or more applications on-screen at one time, so you can easily compare or share the information between the applications.

Windows provides several methods of sharing data between applications: copying, moving, and linking. Suppose you create a spreadsheet of quarterly sales and you want to use the figures in a report to your boss. You can use any of the sharing methods to accomplish this task.

You can select and copy the data in the spreadsheet application and then switch to the word processing application that holds the text of the report. Paste the data and format it like you would any other text. The original data remains in the spreadsheet program for later use and it also appears in the report.

You can move the text from the spreadsheet program to the report, if you no longer need it in the original program or file. Selecting and cutting the data removes it from the spreadsheet program and places it on the Clipboard—an area in Windows set aside for holding copied or cut material. Material stays on the Clipboard until you cut or copy something else; you can paste material from the Clipboard over and over again. From there, you can paste it to the report in the word processing program.

Finally, you can provide a link between the spreadsheet and the report that updates the data automatically whenever you change it in the spreadsheet program. Using OLE (Object Linking and Embedding), you can make sure your work is always current and accurate.

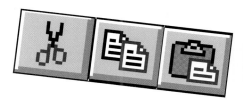

Windows applications that support OLE enable you to tie together documents between two applications, or between the source and destination. You create the data in the *source*, for example a spreadsheet program. You then create a *link* between the source and the *destination*, or the report in the word processing program. Now, whenever you change the data in the source, it automatically updates in the destination.

OLE also enables you to share data by *embedding* information instead of linking. When you embed data, you create the data within the destination application using the source application. In the report, for example, you choose the spot in which you want to insert spreadsheet data. Through the Edit menu of the word processing application, you open the spreadsheet program as an "object" and create the spreadsheet within the destination application.

When you complete the spreadsheet, you close the source application and the spreadsheet becomes embedded in the word processing document. When you need to update the data, you can double-click the spreadsheet in the word processing program and the spreadsheet application opens, ready for editing.

This part illustrates how to switch between applications and share data by copying, moving, linking, and embedding.

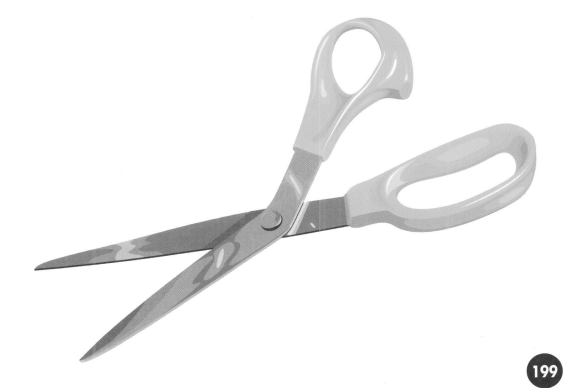

Switching Between Applications

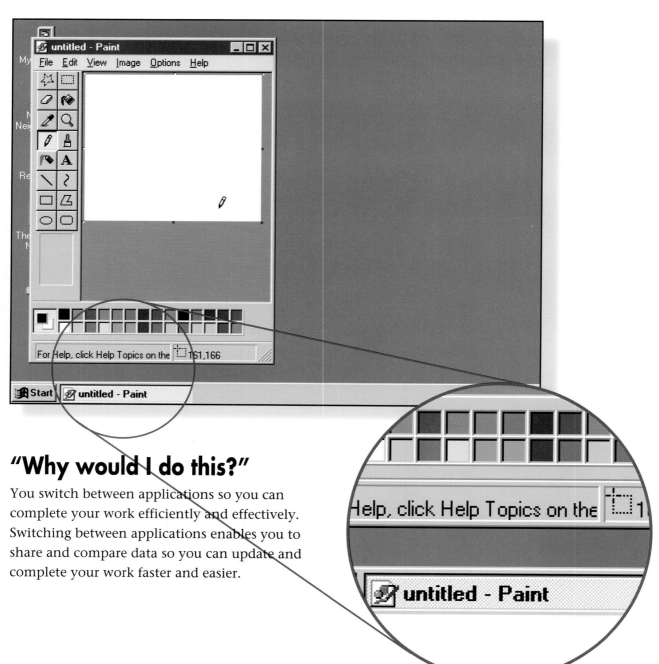

"Why would I do this?"

You switch between applications so you can complete your work efficiently and effectively. Switching between applications enables you to share and compare data so you can update and complete your work faster and easier.

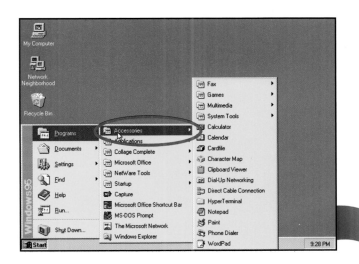

1 From the **Start** menu, open your word processing program. If you do not have a word processing program installed, you can open **WordPad** from the **Accessories** folder. Click the **Minimize** button. Notice the program's icon on the taskbar.

2 From the **Start** menu open a spreadsheet, or other program such as **Paint** or **Cardfile** from the **Accessories** window. Windows displays the second program on-screen and represents it with a button in the taskbar.

NOTE ▼

> The number of programs you can have open at any one time depends on the amount of RAM (random-access memory) in your system.

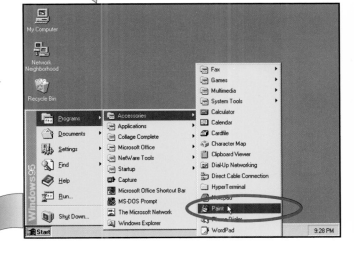

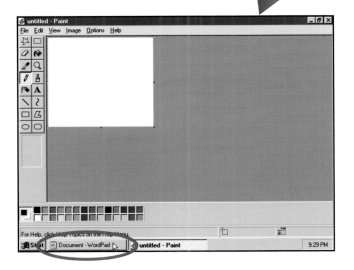

3 To switch back to the word processor, click the program's button on the taskbar. Windows brings the first program forward to display on-screen. ■

WHY WORRY?

> Instead of switching between programs using the taskbar, you can arrange the open application windows on-screen. Point the mouse pointer at an empty spot on the taskbar and press the right mouse button. Choose the Tile Horizontally or Tile Vertically command from the menu that appears.

201

Viewing the Clipboard

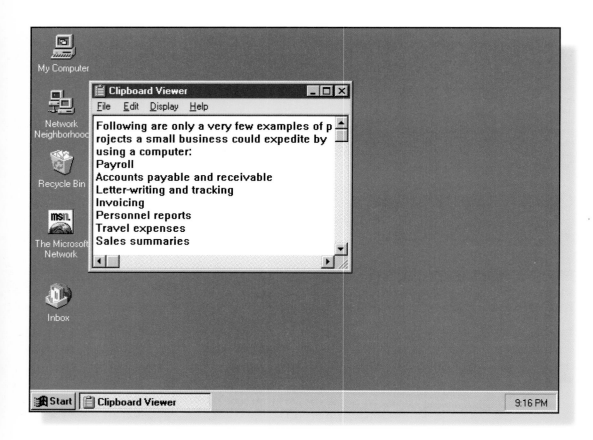

"Why would I do this?"

Use the Clipboard Viewer to view, edit, and save material you cut or copy to the Clipboard. Whenever you choose to cut or copy material in any Windows program, that material is placed on the Clipboard. You can paste the material to another location, document, or application; however, if you choose to cut or copy something else, the material on the Clipboard is replaced. You can use the Clipboard Viewer to save that material and use it another time.

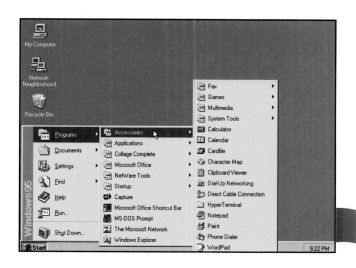

1 Click the **Start** button and choose **Programs**. From the secondary menu, choose **Accessories**; then choose **Clipboard Viewer**. The Viewer's icon looks like a clipboard.

2 If you have cut or copied material during the current session, the Clipboard Viewer window appears with that material. To save the material in a file to itself, choose **File**, **Save As**. The Save As dialog box appears; enter a name for the file in the File Name text box. Clipboard files are saved with CLP extensions in the C:\WINDOWS\DESKTOP folder. Choose **OK** to save the file. You can view the Clipboard file at any time by choosing **File**, **Open** in the Clipboard Viewer and choosing the saved file name. Choose **File**, **Exit** to close the Clipboard Viewer. ■

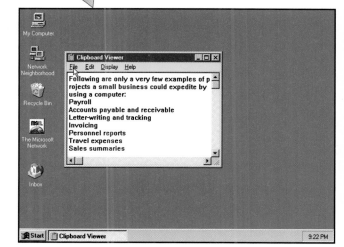

NOTE ▼

If the Clipboard Viewer is not on the Accessories menu, install it by first opening the Control Panel. Double-click the Add/Remove Programs icon. Choose the Windows Setup tab and double-click Accessories in the Components list. The Accessories dialog box appears. In the Accessories Components list, choose Clipboard Viewer and then choose OK. Choose OK to add the Clipboard Viewer. Follow the on-screen directions.

TASK 66
Copying Data Between Applications

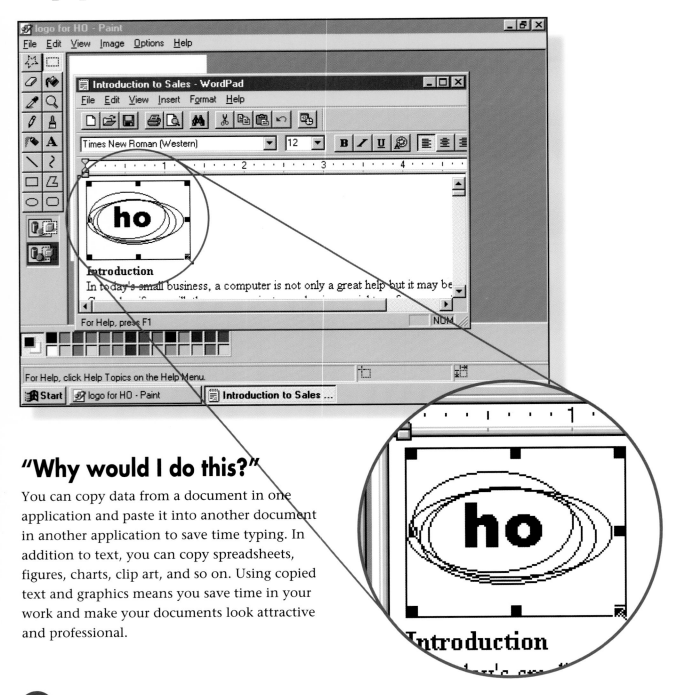

"Why would I do this?"

You can copy data from a document in one application and paste it into another document in another application to save time typing. In addition to text, you can copy spreadsheets, figures, charts, clip art, and so on. Using copied text and graphics means you save time in your work and make your documents look attractive and professional.

204

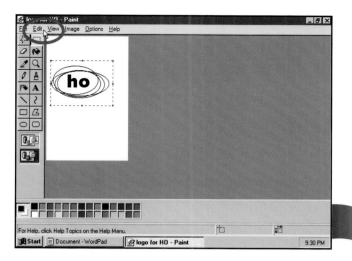

1 Open any two Windows applications and enter data—numbers, text, sound, or graphics—into one of the applications. Select that data. Then open the **Edit** menu and choose the **Copy** command. Windows copies the data to the Clipboard.

> **NOTE** ▼
>
> Instead of using the Edit menu, you can use the keyboard shortcut Ctrl+C to copy.

2 Click the button on the taskbar representing the program you want to switch to. Windows displays the application.

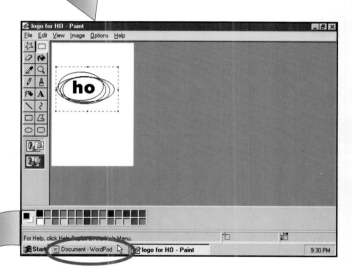

3 Position the insertion point in the document and open the **Edit** menu; choose the **Paste** command. Alternatively, press the shortcut keys **Ctrl+V**. The data is pasted into the document. ■

Moving Data Between Applications

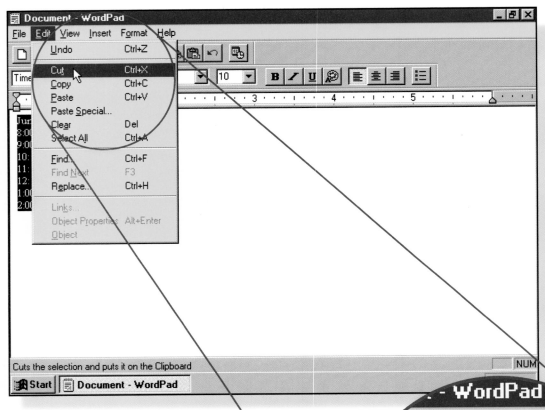

"Why would I do this?"

You can move, or cut, information from one application to another so you can represent it in the proper format. Suppose, for example, you entered tomorrow's schedule in WordPad; however, as you work you want to use an alarm such as the one in the Calendar accessory to notify you when it's time for your first meeting. You can cut the schedule from WordPad and move it to the Calendar accessory, where you can set the alarm.

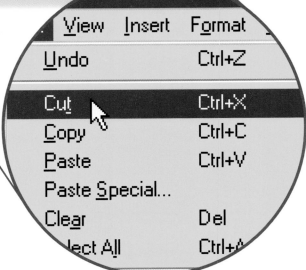

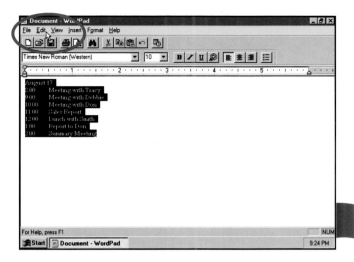

1 Open any two Windows applications and enter data into one of the applications. Select that data. Then open the **Edit** menu and select the **Cut** command.

> **NOTE** ▼
>
> Use the keyboard shortcut Ctrl+X to cut.

2 Click the button on the taskbar representing the program you want to switch to. Windows displays the application.

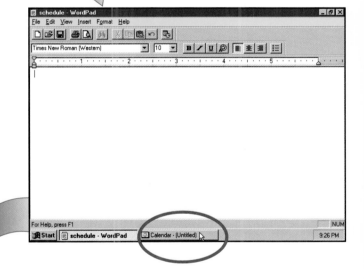

3 Position the insertion point in the document and open the **Edit** menu; choose the **Paste** command. Alternatively, press the shortcut keys **Ctrl+V**. The data is pasted into the document. ■

TASK 68

Linking Data Between Applications

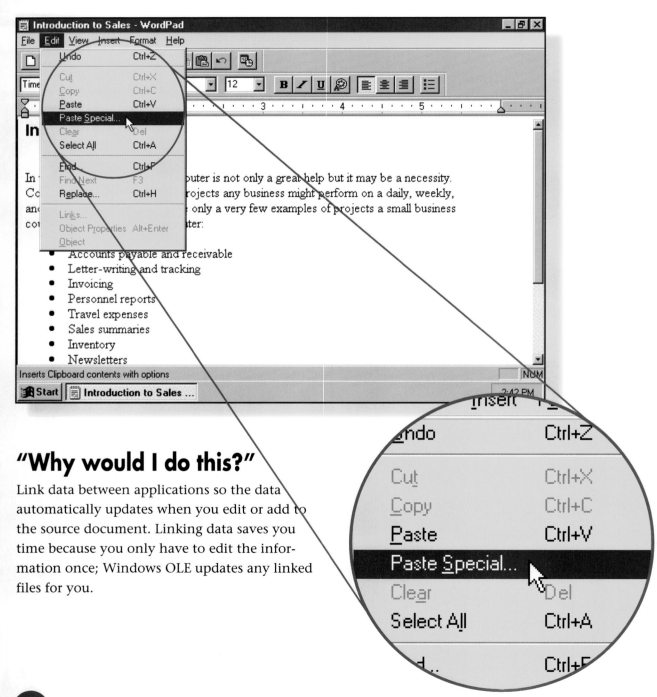

"Why would I do this?"

Link data between applications so the data automatically updates when you edit or add to the source document. Linking data saves you time because you only have to edit the information once; Windows OLE updates any linked files for you.

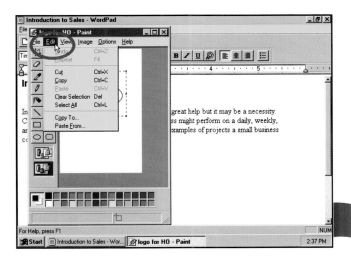

1 In the source document, select the data you want to link and then open the **Edit** menu; choose the **Copy** command. Windows copies the selected data to the Clipboard.

2 In the taskbar, switch to the destination document; alternatively, you can open the application if it is not already open. Position the insertion point where you want the linked data to go and open the **Edit** menu. Choose the **Paste Special** command. The Paste Special dialog box appears.

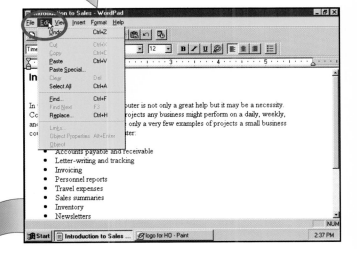

3 Select the **Paste Link** option button, and select the format you want to paste from the list box. The available formats depend on the type of data you're pasting. You can, for example, choose to paste a picture as a Metafile or a Bitmap. Choose a Bitmap file if your printer is a dot matrix, for example, because the structure of a Bitmap object works best with that printer. Choose **OK**. Windows inserts the data with a link between the destination and the source files. ■

Embedding an Object

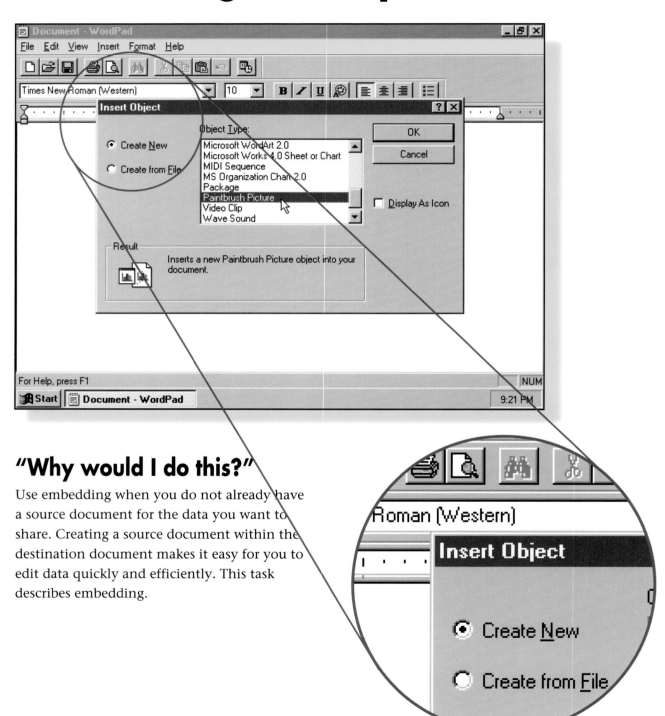

"Why would I do this?"

Use embedding when you do not already have a source document for the data you want to share. Creating a source document within the destination document makes it easy for you to edit data quickly and efficiently. This task describes embedding.

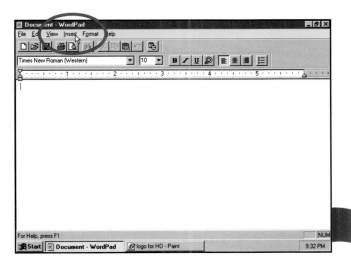

1 In the destination document, position the insertion point where you want the embedded object to go. Then open the **Insert** menu, and choose the **Object** command. The Object dialog box appears. Not all applications' Object dialog boxes look the same but they will be similar. From the list of Object Types, choose the application in which you want to create the data and choose **OK**. The application window opens.

2 Enter the data as you normally would in that application.

> **NOTE** ▼
>
> Not all Windows applications support Object Linking and Embedding; if you cannot find an Insert Object command, check the application's documentation to see if OLE is supported.

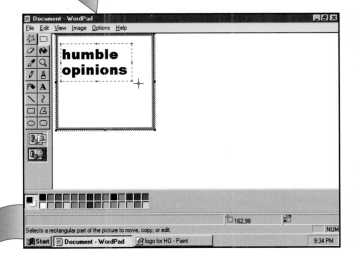

3 When you are done, open the **File** menu. Look for an **Update** command and choose it. Then look for an **Exit** and **Return to Document** command. Sometimes, the two commands are combined. Windows closes the application and embeds the data into the destination document. ■

> **WHY WORRY?**
>
> Any time you want to edit the data in an embedded object, double-click the object.

PART IX
Using Windows Accessories

213

Windows provides several accessories, or applications, you can use to help you in your work. These accessories are not full-blown applications, but they are useful for specific jobs in the Windows environment. Included in the accessories are a calculator, calendar, games, painting program, word processor, and faxing application.

Included with Windows are several games you can play on the computer. Minesweeper and Solitaire are two games traditionally associated with Windows. Solitaire is the card game we all learned as children, and Minesweeper is a game of chance. Additionally, Windows includes FreeCell, Hearts, and Party Line. FreeCell is a variation of the Solitaire game in which you try to make four stacks of the fifty-two cards in order of rank and suit. You can play Hearts, another card game, with the computer or with other people on your network. The object of the game is to get the lowest score. Finally, Party Line is a game played with others connected to your network, involving inventing rumors and passing them from player to player.

Windows also provides a simple word processor called WordPad. WordPad enables you to enter and edit text files, such as the AUTOEXEC.BAT or CONFIG.SYS. Furthermore, you can format text in WordPad using various fonts, type sizes, tab settings, and text alignment. You can even insert objects using OLE. WordPad is limited, however, in that it does not check spelling or allow headers and footers, kerning, and other complex word processing features.

In addition to WordPad, Windows includes a text editor: NotePad. NotePad is a bare-bones word processor you can use to edit basic text files. Additionally, many Windows files are in the NotePad format, such as the help files, readme files, and various other text documents in Windows. You cannot format text in the NotePad but you can print files, search for specific words or phrases, and save and open text documents.

To help you keep your schedule organized, Windows includes a program called Calendar. Calendar provides a "notebook" of sorts, which you can use to enter meetings and important dates. Additionally, the Calendar includes an alarm you set to notify yourself of important meetings.

Occasionally you may need to insert artwork of some type into your documents. Windows' Paint enables you to create and edit drawings, as well as edit clip art, screen captures, and other graphic files. Paint is a basic drawing and painting program that comes in handy for quickly polishing your art works.

Windows provides an application called Fax that enables you to fax files from your computer over a modem to another computer. Additionally, you can create custom fax cover pages and request faxes from fax information services.

Similarly, use the Cardfile to store phone numbers and addresses, just like you would in your Rolodex card file. In Cardfile, you can also print the information on the cards, search for specific names or addresses, and save and open files.

Finally, you can use any of the Windows Multimedia tools to play CDs or other media, such as film clips, and to record and play back sounds to accompany presentations and so on.

The more you work in Windows, the more occasion you will find to use many of the Windows accessories. This part shows you how to open and use the accessories described.

TASK 70

Playing Games

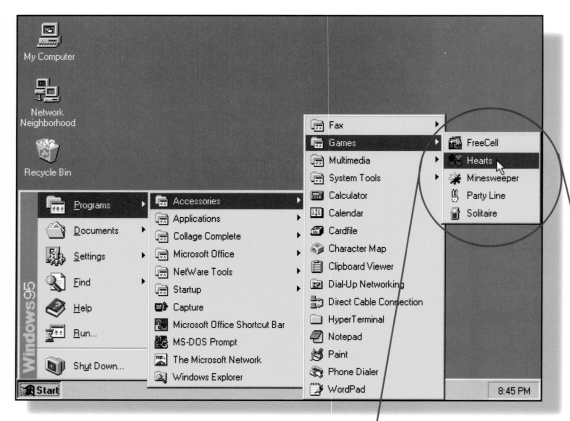

"Why would I do this?"

Windows provides several games you can play
to break your workday with a little entertain-
ment. Use any of the games to fill a lunch hour
or coffee break and to ease the tensions of the
day. This task shows you how to open the
games accessories in Windows.

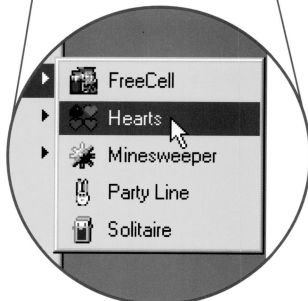

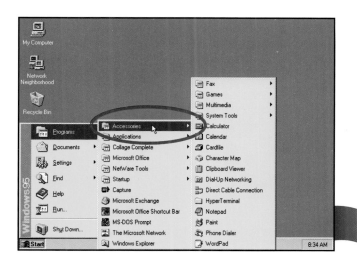

1 Open the **Start** menu and choose the **Programs** menu; then select the **Accessories** folder and the Accessories menu appears. From the Accessories menu, choose the **Games** folder. The Games menu appears. Click the name of the game you want to open, Solitaire for example. The game's window appears.

2 After opening the game, choose the **Help** menu for instructions on how to play the game.

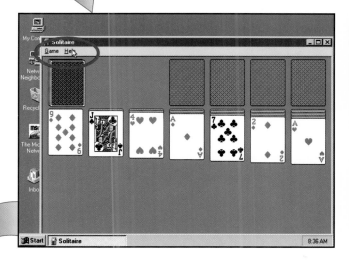

3 To close any game in Windows, click the **Close** button (**X**) in the title bar. ■

217

TASK 71
Controlling Multimedia

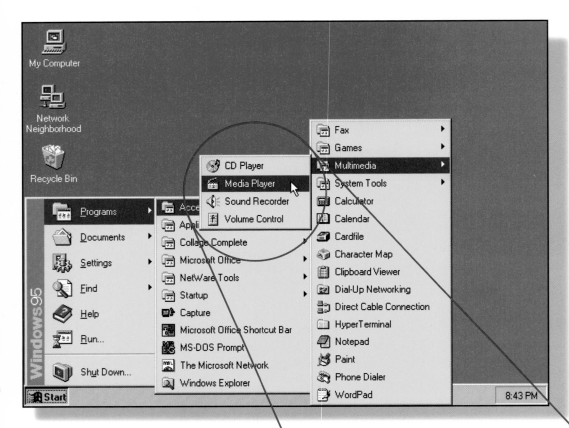

"Why would I do this?"

You can use various Windows multimedia devices, such as the Sound Recorder or Media Player, to add to your presentations or documents you create in Windows. Use the CD player to listen to audio CDs, view film clips with the Media Player, or record your own sounds and insert the sound files into your documents for clarification or interest.

218

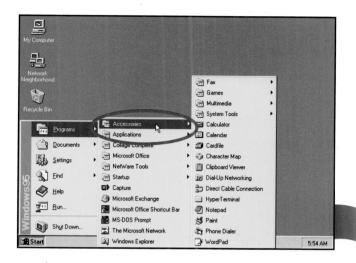

1 To open the Multimedia folder, open the **Start** menu and choose **Programs**. Next, choose **Accessories**, **Multimedia**. The secondary menu appears, containing four options.

2 Choose the **CD Player** from the Multimedia menu. The CD Player window appears. The CD Player works similarly to a CD player in your stereo. You can choose to play, pause, stop, fast-forward, or rewind the CD in the drive. You can choose the tracks you want to play and arrange them in various orders according to the artist or title, if you are set up to play multiple discs. Click the **Close** button to close the CD Player window.

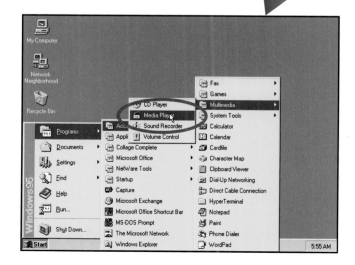

3 Choose **Media Player** from the Multimedia menu to play audio, video, and animation files. You can use the controls at the bottom of the Player to play, pause, stop, fast-forward, rewind, and otherwise control the playback. To close the Media Player, click the **Close** button. ■

Writing and Editing in WordPad

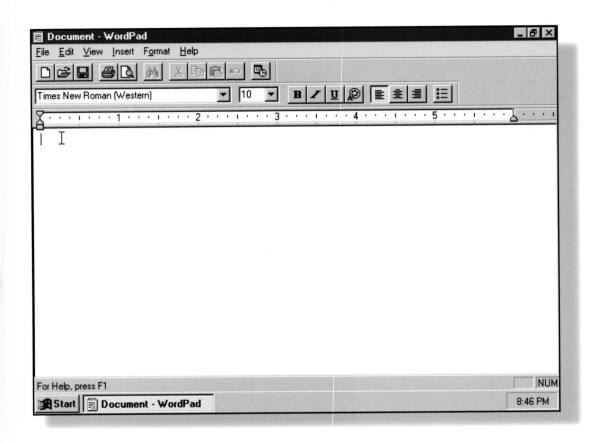

"Why would I do this?"

Use WordPad to edit text files, such as your AUTOEXEC.BAT, or to quickly create formatted text, such as notes, memos, fax sheets, and so on. WordPad saves files in Word 6 for Windows format by default, but you can choose to save in a text-only format when editing configuration files.

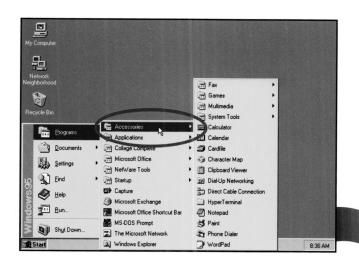

1 Open the **Start** menu and choose the **Programs** menu; then select the **Accessories** folder and the Accessories menu appears. From the Accessories menu, choose the **WordPad** command. The WordPad window appears with a Toolbar, Format Bar, Ruler, and Status Bar ready to help you in your work.

2 Click the **Maximize** button if you want to enlarge the WordPad window for easier working. The blinking cursor in the work area indicates where new text will appear when you type.

> **NOTE** ▼
> To hide any of the screen elements in WordPad, choose the View menu and click the tool you want to hide. A check mark indicates the tool is showing; no check mark indicates it is hidden.

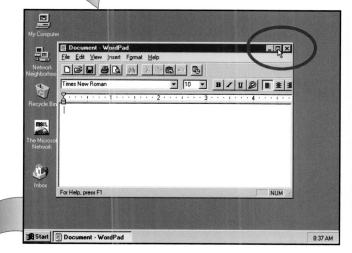

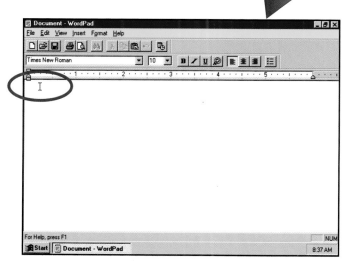

3 Type your name and press **Enter**. Pressing Enter creates a new paragraph by moving the blinking cursor down one line.

> **NOTE** ▼
> If you want to type paragraphs of text, you do not need to press Enter at the end of a line of text to start a new line. WordPad includes automatic text wrap; you only press Enter to start a new paragraph.

4 To change fonts, click the down arrow by the Font box on the Format Bar. Scroll to the top of the list and choose **Arial**. All text you enter from this point will remain in the Arial font until you choose a different font. You can also choose Font from the Format menu to select a new font.

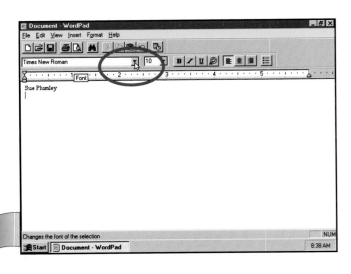

> **NOTE** ▼
>
> The Format Bar also contains a size button; bold, italic, and underline buttons; a font color button; bullet button; and left, center, and right alignment buttons.

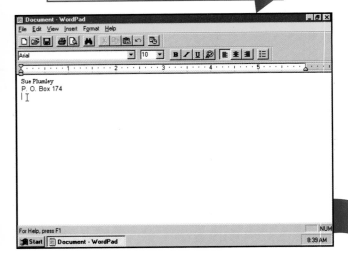

5 Enter your address at the insertion point, or blinking cursor. Press **Enter**. If you make a mistake while typing, press the **Backspace** key to delete one character at a time. Alternatively, you can drag the mouse over any text to highlight the text and then press the **Delete** key to remove the text.

6 To save a file, open the **File** menu and choose the **Save As** command. The File Save As dialog box appears. In Save in, choose a drive and/or folder in which to save the document.

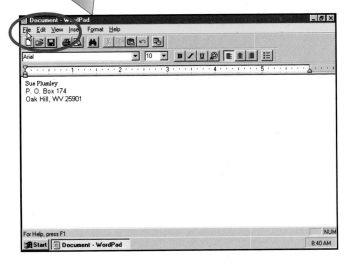

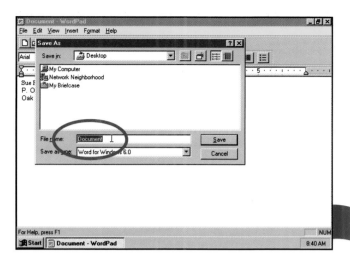

7 In the File Name text box, enter a name for the file, such as Document. You can enter a file name that's up to 255 characters, if you want, to describe your document. Choose **Save** to save the file.

8 To print a document, open the **File** menu and choose the **Print** command. The Print dialog box appears. Choose the **Print Range** and number of copies; then choose **OK** or press **Enter** to print the document.

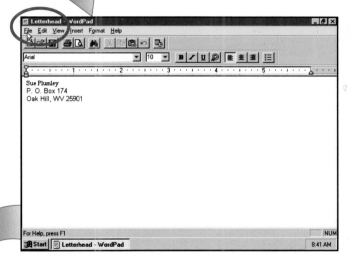

9 To close WordPad, open the **File** menu and choose the **Exit** command; alternatively, click the **Close** button in the title bar of the program. ■

Using the Calendar

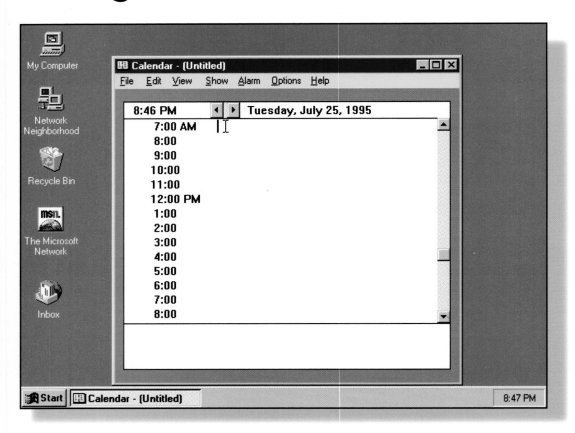

"Why would I do this?"

Use the Windows Calendar accessory to keep your daily schedule and even set an alarm to warn you of an upcoming meeting. This task illustrates how to use the Calendar.

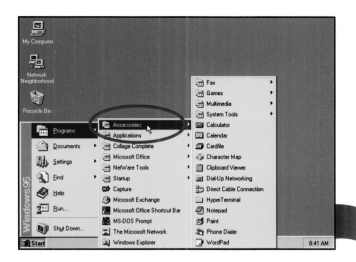

1 Open the **Start** menu and choose the **Programs** menu; then select the **Accessories** folder and the Accessories menu appears. From the Accessories menu, choose the **Calendar** command. The Calendar accessory opens. Position the mouse I-beam after the 10:00 entry and click to position the cursor.

2 Type **Meet w/ Dave-OLPO**. You can click the mouse after any time entry and enter your appointments and schedule. Use the scroll bar to see more time entries.

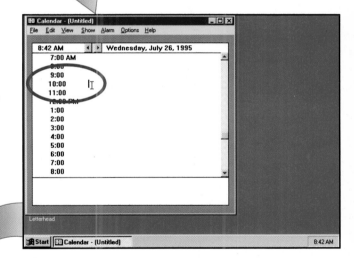

3 To change the day, click the arrows to the left of the current date on the calendar. The left arrow moves back one day and the right arrow moves ahead one day for every click.

WHY WORRY?

If you want to see the entire month, open the View menu and choose Month; alternatively, press F9. To switch back to a daily view, press F8.

4 To set an alarm for the 10:00 meeting, position the cursor on the line of text and open the **Alarm** menu. Choose the **Set** command. A bell appears in the left margin beside the time, indicating the alarm is set.

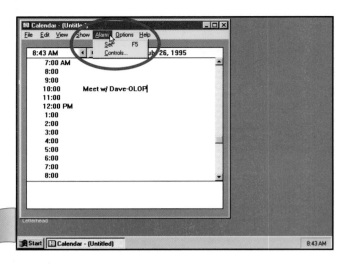

NOTE ▼

To change the alarm settings, open the Alarm menu and choose Controls. You can choose to ring the alarm up to 10 minutes before the meeting. Choose OK to close the Alarm Controls dialog box.

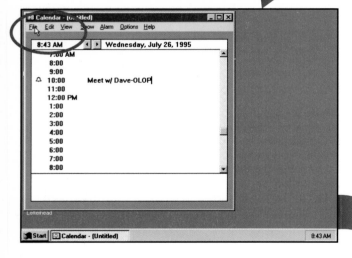

5 To save the calendar, open the **File** menu and choose the **Save As** command. The Save As dialog box appears.

6 Enter the name of the calendar in the File name text box and choose **OK** to save the file. Windows automatically fills in the three-letter extension (CAL) to the file name.

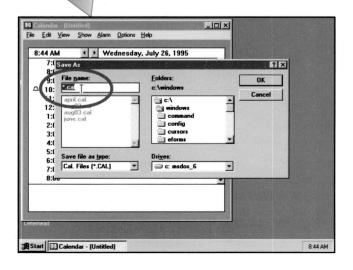

NOTE ▼

You can access a previously saved file by choosing the File menu and the Open command and choosing the file from the File list.

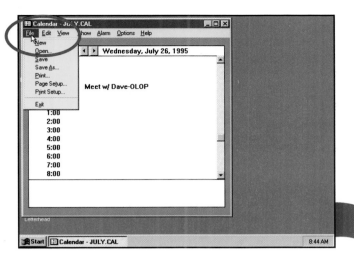

7 To print the calendar, open the **File** menu and choose the **Print** command. The Print dialog box appears.

8 In the From text box, enter the date from which you want printing to begin. In the To text box, enter the date to which you want the printing to end. Choose **OK** to print the calendar.

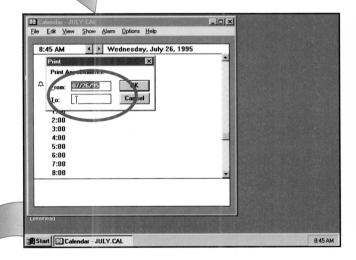

9 To close the Calendar program, open the **File** menu and choose the **Exit** command. ■

TASK 74

Using Cardfile

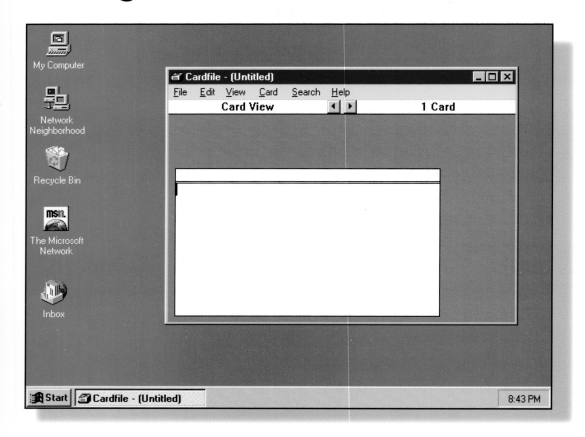

"Why would I do this?"

Use the Cardfile to keep names, addresses, and phone numbers in an organized file that you can save, print, and edit. The Search feature in the Cardfile makes it easy to find specific names or numbers, as well.

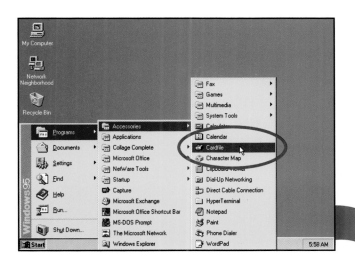

1 Open the **Start** menu and choose **Programs**. Next, choose **Accessories**, **Cardfile**.

2 Begin typing at the insertion point to enter a name, address, and phone number on the card. You can, alternatively, enter other data such as inventory, employee records, and so on.

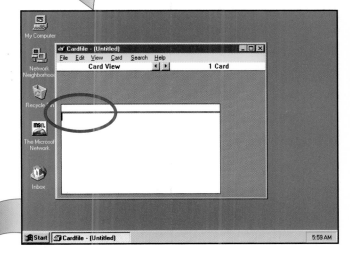

3 To add an index line at the top of the card, choose **Edit** and then choose **Index**; alternatively, you can press **F6**. The Index dialog box appears with the insertion point in the Index Line text box. Enter the text you want to use to index the record and choose **OK**.

4 Choose the **Card** menu and choose **Add to add another card**; alternatively, press **F7** to quickly add a card to the records. Continue to enter data for each card you want to add.

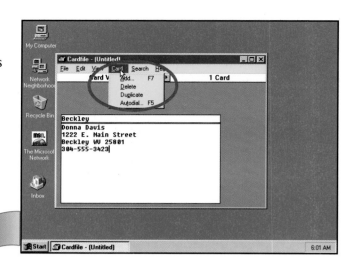

5 To find a specific card, choose **Search** and then **Find**. In the Find What text box, enter the name, street, or other data you want to find. Choose whether to Match Case and in which direction you want to search, and then choose **Find Next**. Cardfile searches the cards and brings the one you're looking for to the front of the stack. Choose **Cancel** to close the Find dialog box.

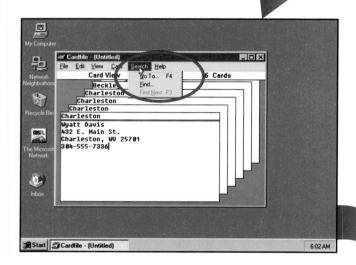

6 To print one card, choose **File**, **Print**. Cardfile prints the selected card. To print all cards in the file, choose **File**, **Print All**.

NOTE ▼
To view only the index lines of each card in a list, choose View, List. Switch back to the card view by choosing View, Card.

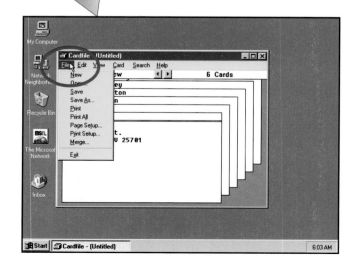

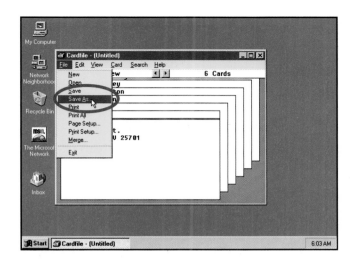

7 To save the card file, choose **File**, **Save As**. Enter the name of the file in the File Name text box and choose **OK**. You can open the saved file at any time by opening **Cardfile**, then choose **File**, **Open** and choose the file name in the list box. To exit the Cardfile, choose **File**, **Exit**. ■

Using Paint

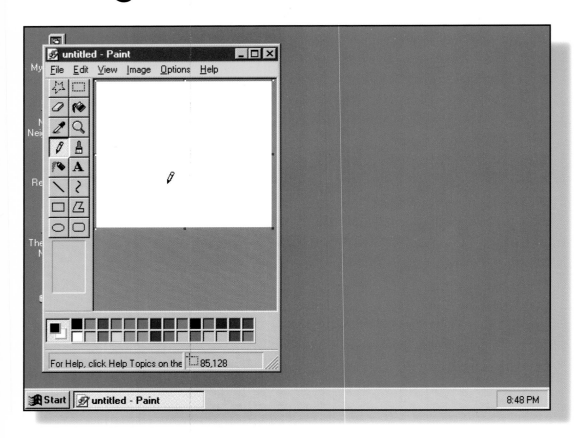

"Why would I do this?"

Use Paint to create art and to edit graphics such as clip art, scanned art, and art files from other programs. You can add lines, shapes, and colors, as well as alter the original components.

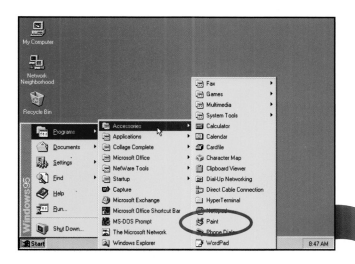

1 Open the **Start** menu and choose the **Programs** menu; then select the **Accessories** folder and the Accessories menu appears. From the Accessories menu, choose the **Paint** command. The Paint window opens, with the pencil tool active.

2 Drag the pencil tool around to get the feel for freehand drawing. If you do not like what you just drew, open the **Edit** menu and choose **Undo**.

> **NOTE** ▼
>
> You also can click in the color bar at the bottom of the Paint window to choose a color other than black to use with the selected tool.

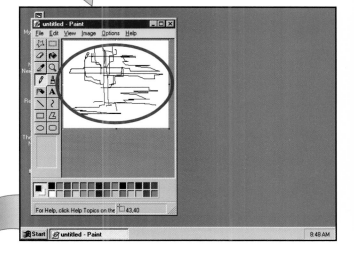

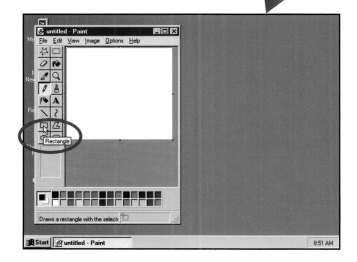

3 On the Toolbar, click the rectangle tool and draw a rectangle in the work area. Click the tool at the point you want the top left corner of the rectangle to be, and then drag the tool diagonally down and to the right to create the shape. You can click any tool on the Toolbar and view a description of the tools in the Status Bar.

4 Click the selection tool from the Toolbar and drag it across part of your drawing. The tool creates a rectangle as you drag, and anything within the rectangle is selected. Press the **Delete** key to remove the selected part of the drawing.

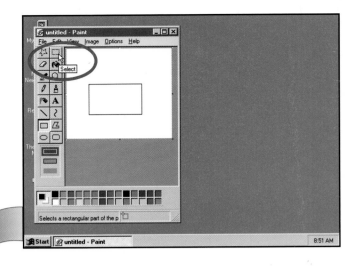

5 To edit an art work in Paint, you must first open it. Open the **File** menu and choose the **Open** command. The File Open dialog box appears. In Look in, choose your hard drive.

6 In the File Name text box, type **C:\WINDOWS\CARS.BMP** and choose **Open** to open the file. Paint displays a dialog box asking if you want to save the changes to the untitled document. Choose **No**. The CARS.BMP file is a Windows bitmap file used for wallpaper. The file opens on-screen.

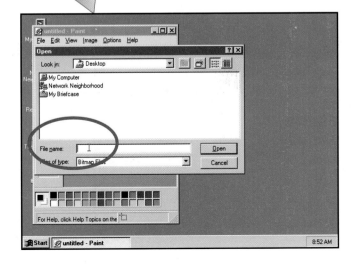

WHY WORRY?

Don't worry about altering the bitmap file; you will not be saving the file so the changes will not be saved.

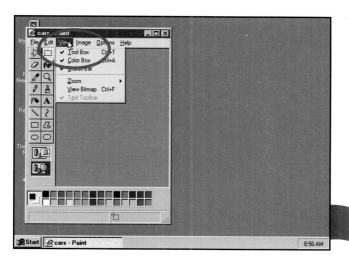

7 Open the **View** menu and choose **Zoom**. A secondary menu appears; choose **Large Size** and the art becomes larger. Using the Paint tools, draw and color the art any way you like.

NOTE ▼

You can click in the color bar at the bottom of the Paint window to choose a color other than black to use with the selected tool.

8 When you finish with the drawing, open the **File** menu and choose the **New** command. Paint displays a message asking if you want to save the file. Choose **No** to cancel the changes.

NOTE ▼

Alternatively, you could choose one of the following commands from the File menu: Save to save the file under the original name; Save As to give it a new name; or Print to print the art.

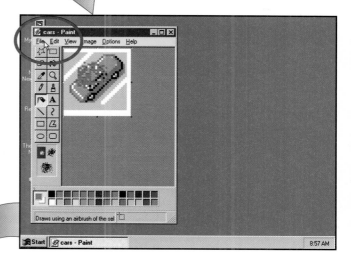

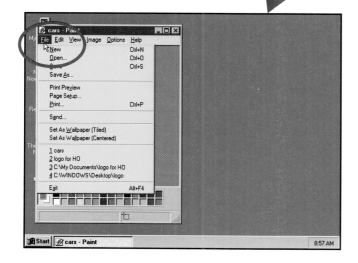

9 To close the Paint application, open the **File** menu and choose **Exit**. ■

TASK 76
Using Microsoft Fax

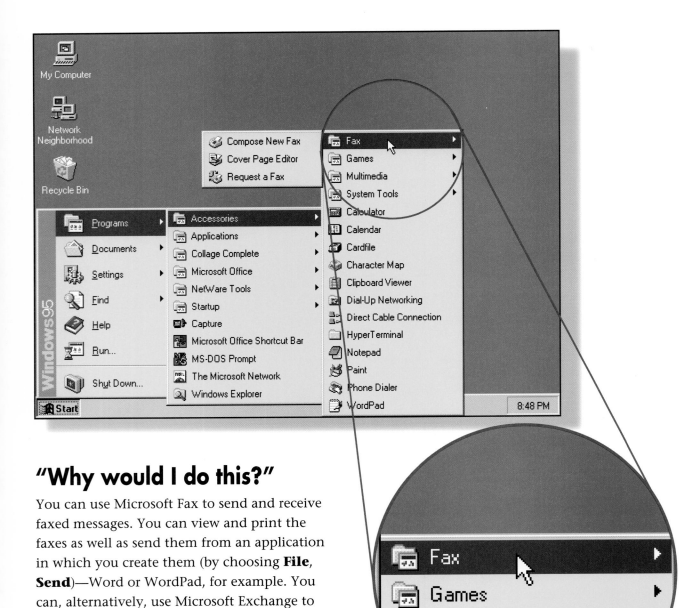

"Why would I do this?"

You can use Microsoft Fax to send and receive
faxed messages. You can view and print the
faxes as well as send them from an application
in which you create them (by choosing **File**,
Send)—Word or WordPad, for example. You
can, alternatively, use Microsoft Exchange to
send faxes or you can use the Fax Wizard. This
task shows you how to send a fax using the Fax
Wizard.

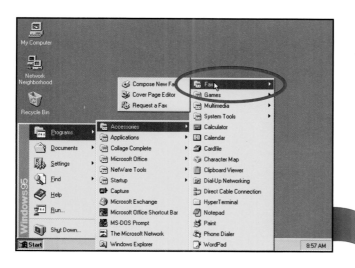

1 Open the **Start** menu and choose **Programs**, **Accessories**, and **Fax**. The Fax menu appears. From the Fax menu, choose **Compose New Fax**. The Fax Wizard box appears.

NOTE ▼

You can choose Cover Page Editor from the Fax menu if you want to create a cover page. Choose the Insert menu in the editor to create the cover page; use the Help menu for more information.

2 The first box names the location from which you're dialing; the default location is your computer. To change any of the Dialing Properties—such as the dialing location, area code, calling card number, and so on, choose the **Dialing Properties** button. Choose **Next** to display the second Compose New Fax dialog box.

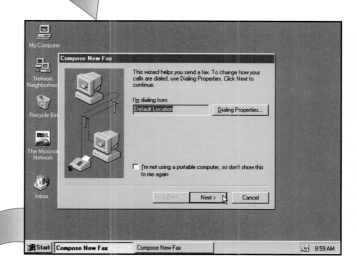

3 Enter the name and fax number of the recipient in the second Fax Wizard box. Choose Address Book to select a name listed in the address book. You can enter new names in the Address Book and choose from those names each time you fax. Choose whether to dial the area code. If you want to send the same fax to two or more people, click **Add to List** and enter another name and number. When ready to continue, click **Next**.

237

4 In the third Fax Wizard box, choose whether to send a cover page. If you choose to send a cover page, select one from the list that best fits your needs. You might choose the Urgent! fax cover page if your message is pressing or choose the For Your Information cover sheet if the fax is incidental. Choose the **Options** button to pick a time to send, add a password, choose paper size, and so on. Choose **Next**.

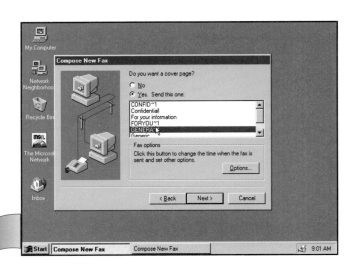

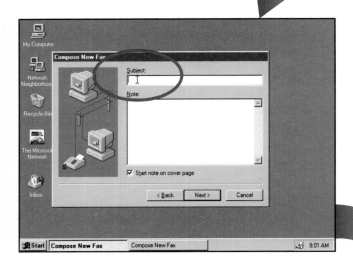

5 The fourth Fax Wizard box presents text boxes in which you can enter the subject and the message. The fax message can be longer than the space shown in the box; simply press **Enter** and continue to type.

6 Choose **Next** and add any files you want to the fax. Choose the **Add File** button to view the files and directories of your computer, choose the file, and return to the fifth Fax Wizard box. If you don't want to add files, choose **Next**. The final Fax Wizard box appears. Choose **Finish** to complete the fax and to let Windows make your call. If you want to cancel the call at any time, click the **Hang Up** button and Windows cancels the fax. ■

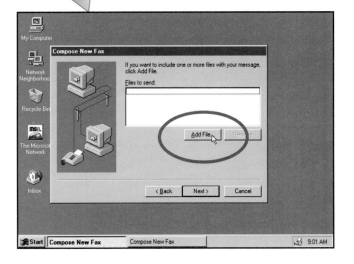

PART X

Maintaining Windows 95

Windows provides many advanced features that enable you to control your applications and files. This last part of the book introduces four advanced techniques you may find useful while working in Windows: installing new hardware devices, defragmenting a disk, scanning a disk for damage, and making and restoring a backup.

Windows makes installing new hardware—such as modems, printers, mice, and so on—relatively easy with hardware Wizards. A *Wizard* is a series of dialog boxes that Windows displays; the dialog boxes give you information and ask questions about the hardware devices.

If you do not know details about your hardware, you can instruct Windows to detect the hardware. Windows then tries to figure out what kind of hardware is attached to your computer, and if it can, it configures the hardware for use without further input from you. If by chance, Windows cannot correctly detect the hardware, you must enter the information manually by checking the documentation that came with the specific hardware you are installing.

Another useful feature included with Windows is the *Defragmenter*. When you save many files to a disk, hard or floppy, your computer stores the files in pieces. Your computer stores some pieces together, consecutively. However, your computer divides and stores other files in pieces on different areas of the disk; these files are fragmented.

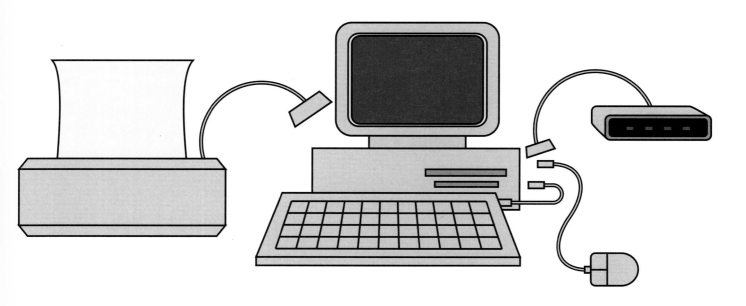

Fragmented files do not normally hurt anything; although, when you access a fragmented file, it takes longer for the computer to find all of the pieces. The Windows *Defragmenter* helps to speed access of files on your computer by consolidating files and storing them in contiguous units.

Another problem Windows can help you with is disk damage. Windows provides a program—*ScanDisk*—that enables you to check your hard disk for damage and can often retrieve data from damaged areas of the disk. In addition to scanning the disk and reporting damage, ScanDisk generates a log of the results so you can view details of the various areas scanned.

In the list of advanced tasks covered in this part of the book is a special feature called *Plug-and-Play*. Plug-and-Play is a method of installing new hardware devices, such as a modem, mouse, printer, sound card, or other cards you add to your computer. Plug-and-Play is a detection device installed in Windows that automatically installs new devices when you turn the computer on.

Use the Backup feature to back up your files on the hard disk to floppy disks, a tape drive, or another computer on your network. After you create backup files, you can restore the files if the originals are lost or damaged.

This part describes how to use these advanced features.

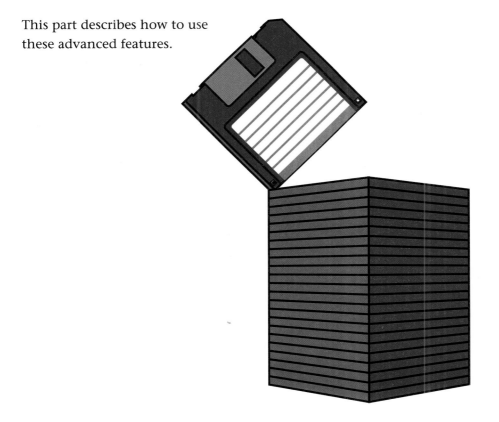

Installing Hardware

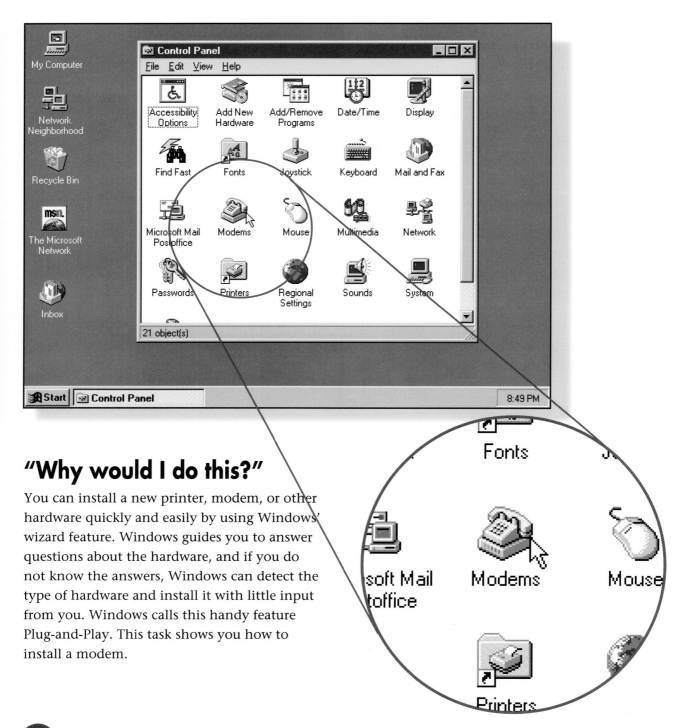

"Why would I do this?"

You can install a new printer, modem, or other hardware quickly and easily by using Windows' wizard feature. Windows guides you to answer questions about the hardware, and if you do not know the answers, Windows can detect the type of hardware and install it with little input from you. Windows calls this handy feature Plug-and-Play. This task shows you how to install a modem.

1 Connect the modem to your computer. Open the **Start** menu, choose **Settings**, and then choose **Control Panel**. In the Control Panel window, double-click the **Modems** icon. The first Wizard box appears.

2 Follow the directions and make a choice to identify the hardware in each Install New Modem box. Choose **Next** when you're ready to move to the next box. You can choose **Cancel** at any time to stop the process.

NOTE ▼

If the hardware is a printer, open the Printer window; if it's a mouse, open the Mouse window. To install controllers, display adapters, sound or video cards, and so on, choose the Add New Hardware icon in the Control Panel.

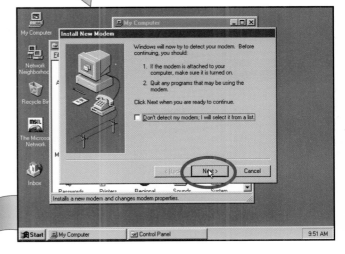

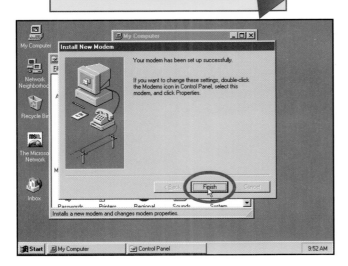

3 When Windows finishes installing the modem, it displays the Modems Properties dialog box listing the device. Choose **Close** to close the dialog box. ■

Defragmenting a Disk

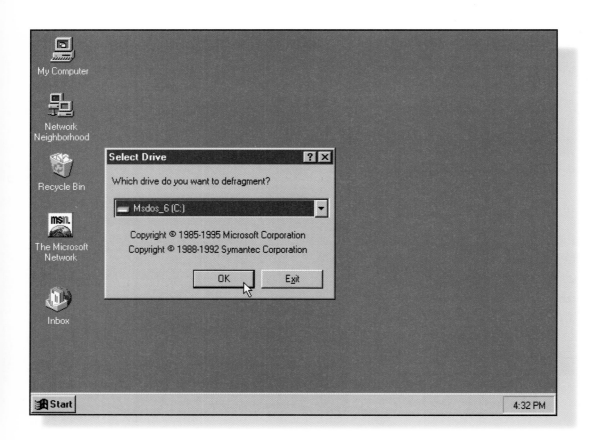

"Why would I do this?"

You can defragment your hard disk to speed
access of files and to help prevent prospective
problems with fragmented files. Defragmenting
your disk is a good, general maintenance job
you should perform every few months for best
results.

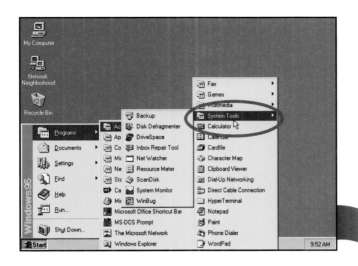

1 Open the **Start** menu and choose **Programs**, **Accessories**, **System Tools**, and finally, **Disk Defragmenter**. The Select Drive dialog box appears.

2 You can defragment your hard drive or a disk in a floppy drive. Select the drive you want to defragment from the drop-down list and choose **OK**. The Defragmenter begins to work.

NOTE ▼

If the disk does not need to be defragmented, Windows displays a message stating you can exit or defragment anyway.

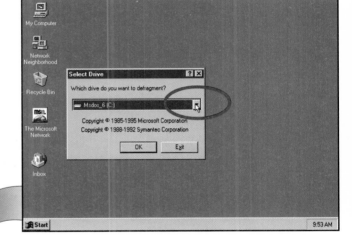

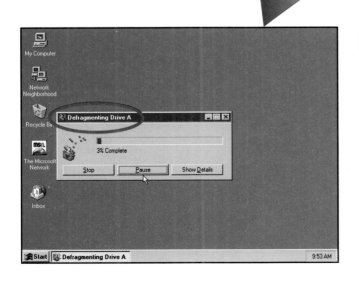

3 As the Defragmenter works, its progress appears in the disk Defragmenter window. You can stop or pause the defragmenting at any time by clicking the appropriate button. When the Defragmenter finishes, a dialog box appears stating it is done and asking if you want to quit Disk Defragmenter. Choose **Yes** to quit or choose **No** to return to the Select Drive dialog box and defragment another disk. ■

Scanning Your Disk

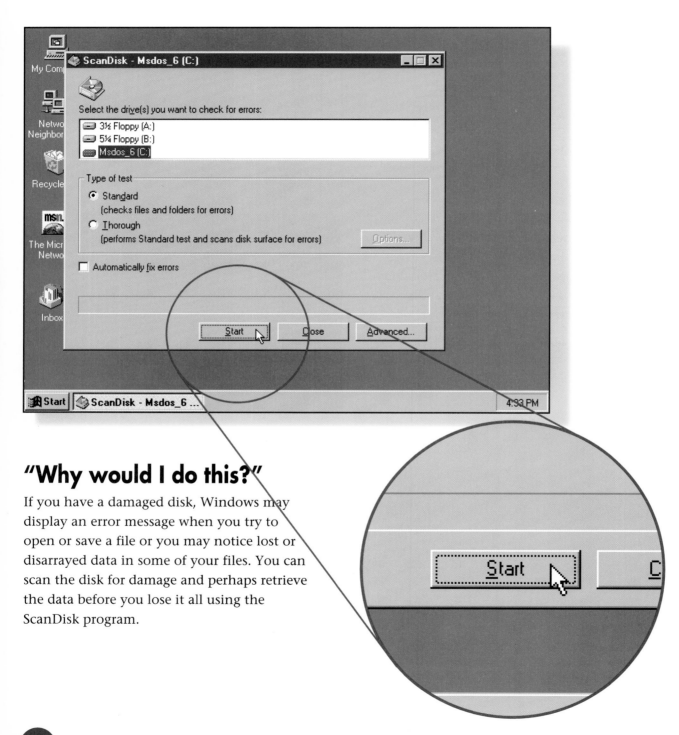

"Why would I do this?"

If you have a damaged disk, Windows may display an error message when you try to open or save a file or you may notice lost or disarrayed data in some of your files. You can scan the disk for damage and perhaps retrieve the data before you lose it all using the ScanDisk program.

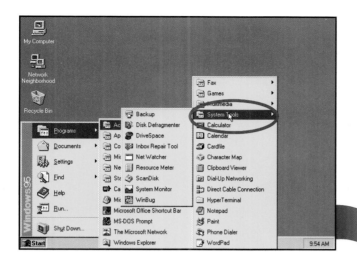

1 Open the **Start** menu and choose **Programs**, **Accessories**, **System Tools**, and **ScanDisk**. The ScanDisk dialog box appears.

2 Choose the drive you want to scan. Choose the type of test you want: **Standard** or **Thorough**. Then choose whether to automatically fix errors. Choose the **Start** button and ScanDisk scans the selected disk.

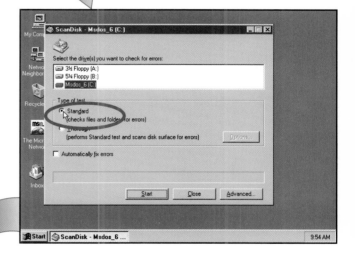

3 If ScanDisk finds an error, a dialog box appears explaining the error. Read the error message and choose the option that best suits your needs. Choose **OK** to continue.

249

4 Answer any other error messages that appear. If the disk is badly damaged, ScanDisk may not be able to correct the errors. If this happens, try running a Thorough test.

NOTE ▼

If you think a disk might be extremely damaged, try running the Defragmenter on it before you use ScanDisk; this may eliminate some of the errors.

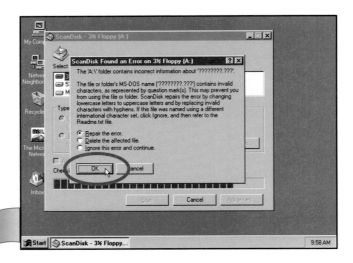

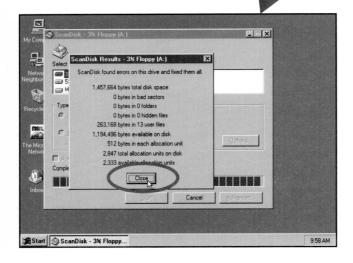

5 When ScanDisk finishes, it displays a report of the scan. Choose **Close** when you're ready to return to the ScanDisk dialog box. Click the **Close** button to exit ScanDisk. ■

TASK 80
Making a Backup

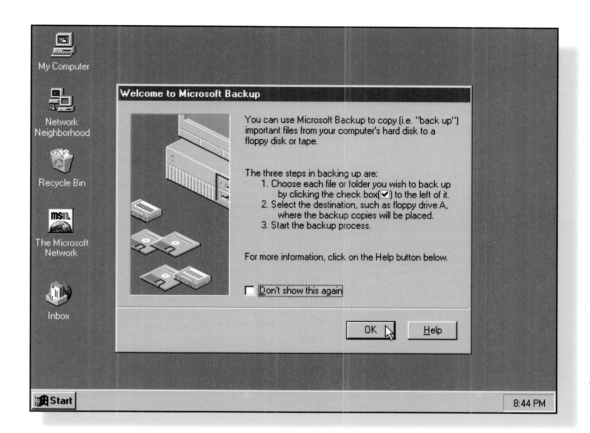

"Why Would I do this?"

Use Microsoft Backup to copy important files to a tape drive or to floppy disks. If your original files are damaged—from lightning or power surges, for example—you can restore the backup files to your computer and continue your work without delay.

251

1 Open the **Start** menu and select **Programs**. Next, choose **Accessories**, **System Tools**. Select the **Backup** command from the System Tools menu.

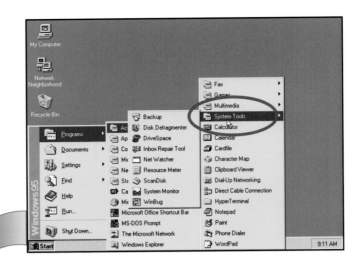

2 The Welcome dialog box appears, explaining the three steps to making a backup. After reading the information, you can choose to not show the dialog box again by checking the option. Choose **OK** to continue the backup.

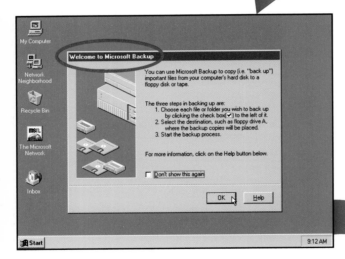

3 A Microsoft Backup dialog box appears giving you information about the backup. Read the box, and if you want, choose the **Don't show this again** option. Choose **OK** to continue.

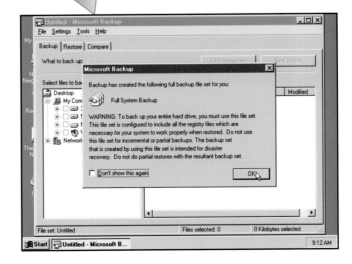

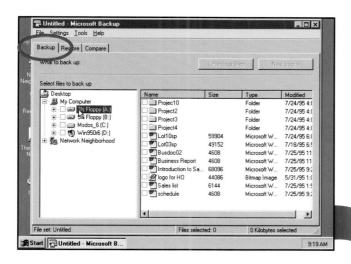

4 In the **Backup** tab, choose the drive you want to back up on the left side of the window. You can select the entire hard disk or just specific folders from the disk; or you can choose to back up data on a floppy drive, CD drive, and so on. When you select a drive, the files and folders appear on the right side of the window.

5 On the right side of the window, select the files you want to back up by clicking the check box in front of the file. A check mark appears in the box to indicate you have selected the file.

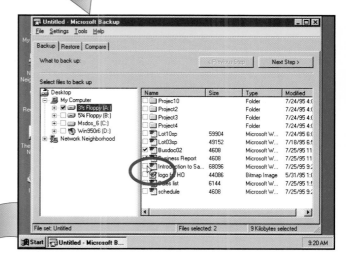

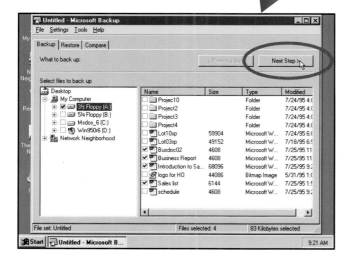

6 Click the **Next Step** button to select where you want to send the backup files. You can choose to send the files to a floppy drive, CD or tape drive, or to another computer, if you're connected to a network. If you choose to back up to the hard drive, double-click the hard drive to display the list of folders.

7 Select the folder you want to back up the files to. Choose **Start Backup** to begin.

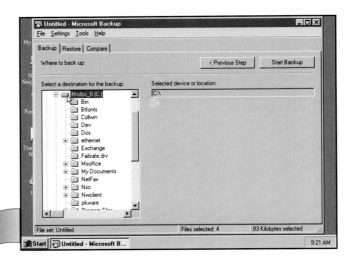

8 The Backup Set Label dialog box appears. In the Backup Set text box, enter a name for the backup set or file that contains your backup data. You can choose **Password Protect** if you want to add a password to the backup so that only someone with the password can restore it. Choose **OK** and Backup begins.

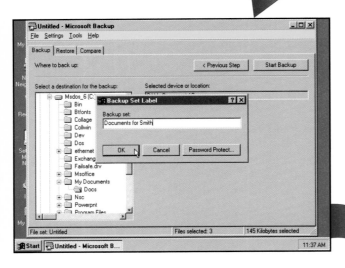

9 When Backup finishes, it displays a message box telling you the Operation is complete. Choose **OK** and then choose **OK** again in the Backup dialog box to return to the Microsoft Backup dialog box. You can close the dialog box by clicking the **Close** button in the title bar. ■

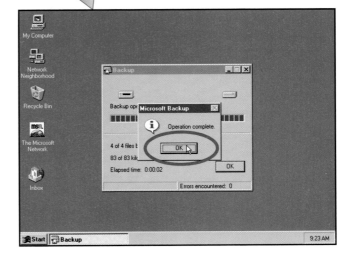

Restoring a Backup

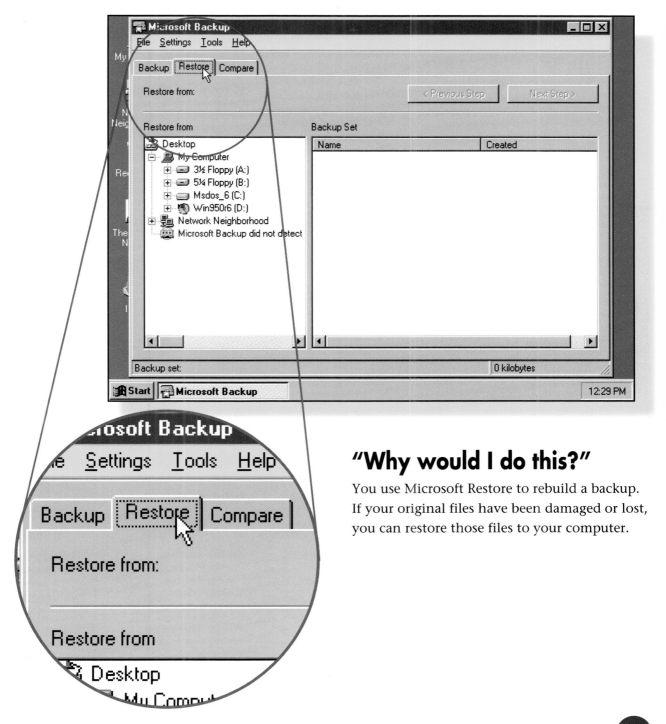

"Why would I do this?"

You use Microsoft Restore to rebuild a backup. If your original files have been damaged or lost, you can restore those files to your computer.

1 Open the **Start** menu and select **Programs**. Next, choose **Accessories**, **System Tools**, and **Backup**.

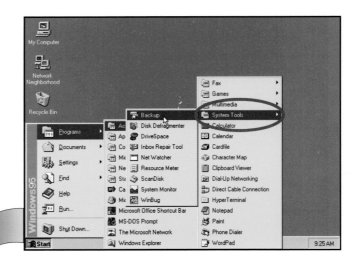

2 Choose the **Restore** tab. In the Restore from list, choose the disk or folder on which you stored your backup files. If you saved the backup to a folder on your hard drive or to another computer, double-click the drive and then open the folder to display the saved file set.

3 On the right side of the Restore window, select the saved backup set and choose the **Next Step** button. The Files to Restore window appears.

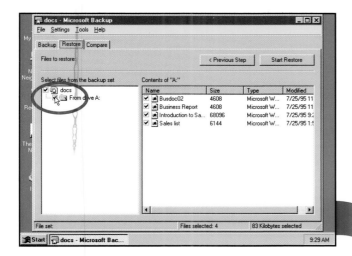

4 On the left side of the window, choose the backup set you want to restore. On the right side of the window, select the files you want to restore. If you click a file that's already selected, you deselect the file.

5 Choose the **Start Restore** button. Backup begins restoring the files. An animated Restore dialog box appears showing the progress.

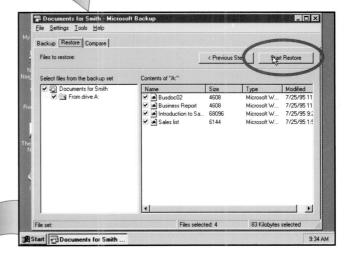

6 When Restore finishes, it displays the complete dialog box. Choose **OK** to close the dialog box and return to the Microsoft Backup dialog box. Click the **Close** button to close the box. ■

NOTE ▼

If Restore detects errors in the process, it displays a dialog box telling you errors were found. You can view the errors by selecting Yes in the message dialog box. You may want to use ScanDisk on the selected drive before trying to restore the files again.

Index

Symbols